A
6
8
4

4

Making Do Without Salt

Making Do Without Salt

Janet Horsley

PRISM PRESS

Published in 1984 by
PRISM PRESS
Stable Court
Chalmington
Dorchester
Dorset DT2 OHB

Copyright © 1984 Janet Horsley

ISBN 0 907061 60 5 Hardback
ISBN 0 907061 61 3 Paperback

Printed by Purnell and Sons (Book Production) Limited
Paulton, Bristol, Great Britain

Contents

Introduction

Salt has become one of the most important taste enhancers used by food manufacturers, cooks and diners to improve the palatability of food. Unfortunately, it is added to so many foods, and in such quantities, that not only does it mask subtle flavours but it is also believed to be detrimental to good health.

Restricting our consumption of salt, however, is easier said than done, for most people become accustomed to salting their food at a very early age and gradually acquire a liking for its taste. Simply omitting salt from our diet gives rise to cries of 'bland', 'boring' and 'tasteless'. When adopting a low-salt diet it is necessary to take a little more care when seasoning food and to make full use of spices, herbs, aromatics and flavourings, which are now readily available from almost every country of the world. I hope this book will encourage everyone to experiment and discover the real pleasures of salt-free food.

The recipes include some traditional favourites but most are completely original. There are dishes for every occasion, with sections on soups, vegetables and salads, savouries, vegetarian dishes, fish, meat, poultry and game and stocks, sauces and salad dressings. They are all brimming over with flavour and the absence of salt goes unnoticed, even by regular users.

Salt as a Seasoning

It is known that virtually all ancient civilisations had access to salt although for a long time it was costly and prestigious, no doubt due to the problems of transporting such a bulky commodity. In early times salt was used in cleaning, bleaching and dyeing fabrics, in preparing hides and leather and in other primitive chemical processes. It was discovered, more by chance than intent, to have preservative properties and its primary culinary use, in the days before refrigeration, canning and bottling, was in salting foods. Not only was this an excellent method of dealing with surfeits of meat following the killing of a pig, cow, deer or other large animal but it was also useful for preserving smaller perishable items, particularly cheese, butter and vegetables, which were needed to supplement meagre food supplies and to add variety to the diet in the cold dark winter months.

Demand for salt rose gradually until, in the fourteenth century, there occurred a dramatic increase in the amount used, resulting from the discovery of an improved method of salting fish. Salted herrings were very popular, particularly with Roman Catholic communities who, for religious reasons, had to abstain from eating meat on Fridays, certain Wednesdays and Saturdays and throughout Lent. One assumes that in areas remote from supplies of fresh fish, salt cod and salted herrings must have featured in the diet with monotonous regularity.

It would be interesting to know what the fourteenth century cook would think about the modern practice of adding salt to food while it is cooking, as a final adjustment to seasoning before it is served and again by the diner at the table. Far from recommending the addition of salt during cooking, early recipe books devoted many pages to the different ways by which a cook could disguise the excessively salty flavour of dishes made with salt meat and fish. Herbs and exotic spices were the principal seasoning agents and were used to add flavour, largely in order to counteract the saltiness. Repeated rinsing in fresh water was also said to help and in many cases it was necessary to add salt-absorbing ingredients, such as breadcrumbs, flour and dried pulses, to the pot during cooking.

Ever since he began to use salt to preserve and season foods man has gradually developed a strong liking, almost amounting to a craving, for its taste. It has been shown that young children dislike salt almost as much as they dislike alcohol and cigarettes and it is only as they begin to eat a wide variety of foods containing salt that they become accustomed both to its taste and to the habit of seasoning their own food at the table. Although there is no evidence to suggest that we have a physiological need for salt there is plenty to indicate that virtually everyone enjoys its taste in a wide range of foods. Multhauf, author of 'Neptune's Gift', has even described salt as "the primordial narcotic" but perhaps this view is a little excessive!

Saltiness is one of the basic tastes experienced in the mouth, the others being sweetness, sourness, alkaline and metallic tastes, pungency, bitterness and astringency. This does not mean to say that in order to enjoy savoury foods we must season them with salt any more than we have to add sugar to a pineapple or banana in order to appreciate its flavour. Our ability to detect subtle flavours and contrasts in taste seems to be under-estimated by food manufacturers and many cooks; in my opinion seasoning is one of the most neglected aspects of cooking today. Perhaps modern foods are to blame for our heavy reliance on salt and sugar, for many simply do not taste or smell as they should, their essential character having been lost during refining and processing. Standardisation, cost considerations and convenience now take precedence over flavour and quality.

One has only to browse through old cookery books and herbals to realise how many aromatic seasonings have fallen into disuse, ousted by cheaper and more convenient synthetic flavourings which the food manufacturers can always rely upon to produce the 'perfect' product. Even so these artificially flavoured foods still have to rely heavily on 'taste enhancers' such as salt, monosodium glutamate and sugar to make them acceptable and palatable to the consumer. I think that it is time to re-educate our palates in appreciating the virtually limitless range of taste sensations, not simply those of saltiness and sweetness. Sadly, in spite of the fact that we have at our disposal a huge and often bewildering array of fresh products, exotic spices, herbs, aromatics and flavourings from almost every country of the world, many people still maintain that salt-free food is tasteless and bland. They justify their desire for salt in terms of physical need and I am regarded as something of a freak because, for reasons of luck rather than good sense, I have never wanted to add salt to my food. In spite of my 'deprivation' and the fact that I indulge in regular strenuous exercise I am still reasonably sound in mind and body which strengthens my view that added salt is unnecessary for good health.

Breaking the salt habit is not always easy and at first you may find that the taste of many foods, without their customary pinch of salt, seem a little flat. I must admit that I did not appreciate this fact until I started to cook professionally and to give demonstrations. It came as quite a blow to my confidence to hear several members of my first audience remarking that some of my dishes were rather bland and needed salt. I immediately began to take greater care with the balance of flavours and with the seasoning, using all manner of herbs, spices and natural flavourings, including freshly ground black pepper, several types of mustard and vinegar, tomato purée, fresh lemon juice, natural yoghurt and sour cream. The lack of salt in my food now goes unnoticed, even by regular salt users, as does the absence of a salt cellar on my dining room table.

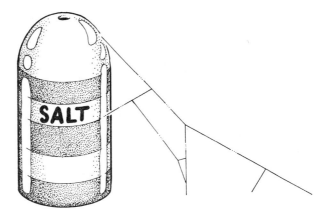

A Question of Health

The act of sprinkling a little salt over one's food to enhance its flavour may seem of so little consequence that it is hard to imagine that it has a significant effect on our health. However, it is generally accepted in medical circles that this pure, innocuous looking substance is a contributory factor in high blood pressure (hypertension), coronary heart disease, strokes, some kidney disorders and oedema (water retention). Perhaps the phrase, 'pure, white and deadly' coined by Professor John Yudkin in reference to refined sugar should also be applied to salt.

High blood pressure is common in western developed countries such as Britain and the United States and is particularly prevalent amongst the elderly. The correlation between rising blood pressure and old age was so well documented in the past that it was assumed to be part of the natural ageing process. However, studies of primitive societies such as the Chinese and Australian Aborigines, the Eskimos, the Polynesians, the Bushmen of the Kalahari Desert, the Masai tribesmen of Tanzania, the Pygmies of the Congo and the Indians of South and Central America has proved otherwise, for each group has been found to have life-long low blood pressure levels.

The most obvious difference between the study groups and the case histories of patients in western countries is the contrast in life styles. The rising incidence of hypertension and heart disease, especially in middle-aged businessmen, was initially blamed on the jet-setting, high-powered, stressful life of western society. Unfortunately, no sooner had the overworked and overweight executive mastered the art of transcendental meditation and purchased a small-holding in the country than new evidence came to light which showed that the incidence of high blood pressure was related to factors other than stress.

While some of the groups with life-long low blood pressure were farmers, some hunters, some simple gatherers, some total vegetarians and others, notably the Eskimos and Masai almost total carnivores, a common factor was that none of them added salt to their food and most had daily sodium intakes of less than 1 gram per day. At first the idea that a substance as common and as apparently innocuous as salt could be responsible for high blood pressure seemed fanciful; after all, one might just as easily say that none of those studied ate caviar or cream doughnuts. However, the apparent link was strengthened by further experiments which provided more evidence to substantiate the theory.

It was found that the cattle-keeping Samburu of Kenya, who ate large quantities of sodium-rich dairy and animal products, maintained life-long low blood pressure in spite of occasional daily sodium intakes in the region of 3-4 grams. However, as soon as their young men were drafted into the Army and began to eat foods liberally seasoned with salt, their sodium levels increased to 15 grams a day followed by a corresponding rise in their blood pressure.

Evidence against salt continued to accumulate until in 1981 H.C. Trowell and D.P. Burkitt in their book, 'Western Diseases: their emergence and prevention' were able to write, 'ethnic groups that do not add common salt to their food have life-long low blood pressure — no exception to this rule has been traced.'

The idea of a possible link between salt consumption and high blood pressure was first mooted at the beginning of the century and up until 1940 low-salt diets were regularly prescribed as a treatment for hypertension and congestive heart failure. In recent years medical authorities have become equally concerned with prevention, and nowadays low-salt diets are used not only as a form of treatment but also as a means of reducing the incidence of high blood pressure and related disorders. In 1975 a report published in the Australian Medical Journal stated that if the average sodium intake of the Australian population were halved the 'epidemic of hypertension' would be prevented. More recently the British Health Education Council, in its attempt to curb the steadily rising incidence of hypertension and heart disease, has stressed the need to eat less salt.

All common salt, whether mined from underground deposits or processed from seawater, is made up of equal parts of sodium and chloride. (One teaspoon of salt consists of approximately 2.5 grams of sodium and 2.5 grams of chloride). Both minerals are essential to good health being vital in ensuring a normal balance of fluid between body cells, in facilitating the movement of nutrients and oxygen into the cells and in aiding the removal of waste products.

Sodium and chloride are found in a wide range of natural foodstuffs and a deficiency is unlikely to occur in a normal diet. The body has no physiological need for added table salt, and sodium in particular is detrimental to good health if taken in excess. The amount of sodium in the body is controlled by the kidneys, which monitor the amount of sodium in the blood and maintain the correct level by retaining or excreting water and sodium as necessary. The mechanism is extremely sensitive, sodium being excreted through the urinary system when intake is high and being conserved when the levels in the body fall. However, this balance may not be maintained without cost, particularly when the diet has included large quantities of manufactured and processed foods, salted butter, salted bread, cakes and biscuits made with baking powder, and liberal amounts of salt added in the kitchen and at the table. High sodium intake requires the kidneys to retain water in order to dilute the concentration in the blood. This results in an increase in the volume of blood in the blood vessels and in the amount of fluid passing into the cell tissues and can cause or aggravate high blood pressure.

A typical western diet includes 8-15 grams (1½-3 tsps) of salt contained in regular daily meals. This figure does not take account of snacks eaten between meals, and some put the actual level of salt intake as high as 25 grams a day. In parts of Japan the situation is even worse. There the passion for salted and pickled foods is such that some Japanese consume over 30 grams of salt a day. This represents a sodium intake sixty times greater than the daily bodily requirements. It is no coincidence that the level of hypertension amongst some Japanese is double that of more modest salt consumers.

Because of the strong links between sodium and hypertension, certain authorities would like to see it banned, at least from processed foodstuffs. There are some, however, who resist such a ban because of a potentially valuable function of salt in the diet. There is a possibility that the body needs extra sodium, in the form of common salt, in tropical climates. It has always been assumed that heat exhaustion and muscular cramps following strenuous exercise in hot climates are due to heavy losses of sodium through perspiration.

Once again, studies have revealed details that bring into question traditional theories. Primitive tribes-people, living in the Tropics and carrying out strenuous physical work, do not suffer from heat exhaustion in spite of the fact that they do not supplement their natural diet with any form of common salt. Similarly experiments carried out on soldiers of the Israeli army, engaged in desert manoeuvres, have shown dietary salt to be unnecessary. Tests revealed that the need for fluid was far more important than that for sodium. As for replacing the sodium lost in perspiration, the soldiers on a low-sodium diet perspired just as freely as their 'salty' colleagues but their sweat was made up of almost pure water. The lack of added salt in their diet meant that there was little excess sodium in the body and therefore less to be excreted in the urine and sweat. The sodium intake from natural dietary sources was found to be sufficient for all physiological requirements, the correct level within the blood being maintained by the kidneys. However, it was found that the soldiers needed time to adjust to a low-sodium diet, and anyone accustomed to eating a diet high in added salt is not advised to reduce their salt intake dramatically or suddenly while actively working in very hot conditions.

It is not surprising that dietary sodium levels in western developed countries are so high for there are three main sources in a typical diet:

1. foods to which salt is added in the kitchen and at the table
2. foods to which salt has been added as a flavouring or preservative, or in raising agents — cheese, bread, self-raising flour, baking powder, butter, pickles, cornflakes, yeast extract, potato crisps, salted peanuts and most processed and tinned foods
3. foods which naturally contain high levels of sodium — meat, poultry, fish, milk and eggs.

A comprehensive list of foods containing sodium is shown on pages 11–15.

A diet with no added table salt, monosodium glutamate, baking powder, sodium sulphite (a preservative used for fruit and vegetables) or sodium nitrate (a preservative used in canned meats) and only modest servings of cheese, eggs, milk, meat, fish and poultry will still contain

between 2–3 grams of sodium a day, equivalent to
that found in one teaspoon of table salt. Even this
amount is five times greater than our daily
requirements but it lies just within the limits
tolerated by the body. Above this level blood
pressure increases steadily, becoming most
noticeable in old people.

THE SODIUM CONTENT OF FOODS — a checklist of ingredients
Low sodium foods contain less than 10 mg per 100 grams.
Medium sodium foods contain between 10–100 mg per 100 grams.
High sodium foods contain over 100 mg per 100 grams.
1000 mg = 1 gram.

Vegetables

Low	Medium	High
artichokes	beansprouts	baked beans
aubergines	broccoli	beetroot
brussels sprouts	cabbage — red	raw celery
cabbage — white	cabbage — spring	spinach
cauliflower	carrots	tinned vegetables
chicory	celery — boiled	certain brands of tomato
courgettes	cucumber	purée and tomato juice
eggplant	all dried beans,	
French beans	pulses and lentils	
green beans	mushrooms	
leeks	mustard and cress	
lettuce	new potatoes	
mange-tout	radishes	
old potatoes	scallions	
onions	spring onions	
parsnips	watercress	
peas	tinned tomatoes	
peppers		
pumpkins		
snap beans		
tomatoes		
zucchini		

Cook all fresh vegetables without salt, soda or salted butter. Always read the labels of canned products and only use those free from added salt — this applies especially to tinned tomatoes, tomato purée and tomato juice. Frozen vegetables are generally salt-free — even so I only use them in emergencies as the taste and texture of fresh vegetables is so much better, although I find frozen peas quite acceptable in most curried dishes.

Fruit and Nuts

Low	Medium	High
almonds	apricots — dried	olives in brine
apples	cashew nuts	all salted nuts
apricots — fresh	chestnuts	peanut butter — salted
bananas	coconuts	
brazils	currants	
dates — fresh and	figs — dried	
dried	prunes	
figs — fresh	raisins	
grapefruit	sesame seeds	
grapes	sultanas	
hazel nuts	sunflower seeds	
lemons	tahini	
lemon juice		
limes		
peanut butter — unsalted		
oranges		
peanuts — unsalted		
pears		
pine kernels (pignoli)		
walnuts		

A recipe for salt-free peanut butter is given on page 58.

Flours and Grains

Low	*Medium*	*High*
brown rice	home-made pasta	flour sifted with
buckwheat		baking powder
bulgar		self-raising flour
couscous		
maize meal		
millet		
oat flakes		
oatmeal		
porridge oats		
soya flour		
unbleached white flour		
wholewheat flour		

When making cakes, biscuits etc. use a sodium-free baking powder — a good chemist should be able to make it up for you.

Sodium-free baking powder:	potassium bicarbonate	38.8 g
	starch	28.0 g
	tartaric acid	7.5 g
	potassium bitartrate	56.1 g

Use half as much again as ordinary baking powder.

Fish

Low	Medium	High
cod	cod's roe	crab
eel	garfish	kippers
halibut	gurnard	lobster
trout	haddock	oysters
herring roe	herring	prawns
	mussels	salt cod
	octopus	scallops
	plaice	smoked fish
	red mullet	tinned fish
	salmon	
	skate	
	sole	
	sprats	
	whitebait	
	whiting	

Meat

Low	Medium	High
	fresh:	bacon
	beef	chicken livers
	chicken	gammon
	duck	kidney
	goose	sausage
	grouse	smoked products
	hare	tinned products
	lamb	tongue
	liver	
	mutton	
	pheasant	
	pigeon	
	pork	
	rabbit	
	turkey	
	veal	

Rabbit has the lowest sodium content of all meats.

Dairy Products

Low	Medium	High
butter — unsalted	cottage cheese — unsalted	butter — salted
vegetable oils	cream cheese — unsalted	all cheeses
	cream	eggs
	egg yolks	margarine
	milk	
	yoghurt	

Unsalted butter does not have the same keeping qualities as salted butter. Buy regularly and keep cool.

Approximately two-thirds of the sodium present in an egg is contained in the white. When following a strict low-sodium diet only use the yolk to thicken sauces and soups and to glaze pie crusts.

Miscellaneous Products

Low	Medium	High
bread — unsalted		baking powder
herbs		bicarbonate of soda
mustards — home-made		bread — commercial
spices		chocolate
vinegar		commercial sauces and pickles
wine		cornflakes
yeast — fresh		miso
		mustards — ready-made
		salad creams
		soya sauce
		yeast extract

A recipe for home-made mustard is on page 107. See under the heading Flours and Grains for a recipe for low-sodium baking powder.

Herbs, Spices and Flavourings

The ability to blend flavours is perhaps the most important culinary skill and the key to good cooking. It cannot be learnt from books or cookery schools but comes from personal experience, intuition and a willingness to be adventurous. The success of a great many chefs has been their ability to add unusual flavourings, in unmeasured but critical quantities. Such details are rarely, if ever, given in recipe books because the quantity and even the nature of the flavouring may vary from day to day, depending on the particular strength of flavour of other ingredients, the whim of the chef and the discretion of his palate. It is best to use the quantity of seasoning agents given in recipes as a rough guide and to learn to trust your own taste buds and judgement. Remember that the intention of herbs, spices and flavourings is usually to complement the basic flavours of the main ingredients, rather than to mask them.

Here is glossary of the herbs, spices and flavourings which I have used in the recipe section. I hope it will encourage you and help you to experiment with them. With a little practice you will soon be adding a pinch of this and a dash of that as confidently as any professional cook. Not only will you have mastered the art of good cooking but you will have also rediscovered the true flavour of many foods, hidden for so long beneath a blanket of salt.

Allspice
The taste of allspice is somewhat reminiscent of cinnamon, cloves and nutmeg. However, it is not a mixture of spices but is the dried fruit of a tree native to Central America. Used whole, it is an important ingredient in marinades and pickles and when ground it is frequently used to enhance the flavour of pâtés, sausages, fruit cakes and plum puddings.

Asafoetida
This evil smelling, grey coloured spice comes from a giant fennel plant. I was introduced to it by an Indian friend who assured me that it adds a certain 'je ne sais quoi' to dishes of spiced vegetables and pulses. It is used in very small amounts, is rarely added to meat dishes and is reputed to have a special affinity with fish.

Basil
Basil is a very aromatic herb, with a smell not unlike that of sweet cloves. It prefers a hot humid

climate, growing best on the Italian Riviera. It is used widely around the Mediterranean, particularly in dishes containing tomatoes, aubergines and Mozzarella cheese. The French often throw a few leaves into a ratatouille, while the Italians use it liberally in a superb spaghetti sauce called pesto alla Genovese. The Spanish and Greeks are less enamoured of the flavour of basil and although it grows freely in both countries, it is used mainly to ward off flies.

Bay
Sometimes called sweet bay or bay laurel. The leaves are dark green, glossy and smooth with a strong aromatic smell when crushed. Bay is one of the three herbs used in a bouquet garni, the 'broth posy' used with fish, meat, fowl and in marinades, pickles and preserves. It is also used to add flavour to sweet dishes such as milk and rice puddings. Bay leaves are best used after drying but their flavour fades with age and they should be replaced each year.

Cardamom
Cardamom is a beautifully aromatic spice, exceedingly popular in Sweden of all places, where it is used liberally to flavour sweet pastries and cakes. It is, however, generally thought of as an eastern spice and an essential ingredient in curries and pilaus. Although expensive do not be tempted to buy cheap cardamom pods, particularly those that are bleached white, for they lack flavour and aroma. A dark brown hairy variety, said to resemble hairy cockroaches, should also be avoided. The best pods are pale green or brown in colour. To judge their quality pull open the parchment-like pod; the seeds inside should be strong smelling, glossy, black and slightly sticky. More often than not the whole pod is added to the cooking pot but it is not to be eaten. On occasions when ground cardamom is needed it is best to grind your own seeds as and when needed, for the ground seed soon loses its flavour.

Chives
Chives belong to the onion family but have a much finer flavour than their larger relatives. They are hardy perennials growing in grasslike clumps. The flowers are small, round and pale mauve in colour but are best cut off to keep all the flavour in the leaves. Finely chopped chives are useful both as a seasoning and a garnish, their fresh bright green leaves looking attractive sprinkled over soups, salads and cooked vegetables. Baked potatoes, sour cream and chives is a delicious combination but they also taste good with omelettes and tomatoes.

Cinnamon
In Britain only true cinnamon is allowed to be sold under that name, whereas in many other countries cassia and other inferior varieties of the same family are lumped together under the same label. The flavour of cinnamon is much more delicate than that of its rivals. Use cinnamon sticks or quills in savoury dishes, discarding them before serving, but for sweet dishes ground cinnamon is preferable.

Cloves
These are an important culinary spice but must be used sparingly. Use whole cloves whenever

possible, anchoring them firmly in a small onion or other vegetable during cooking so that they can be removed easily before the meal is served. Biting on a whole clove by mistake is quite a startling experience, though not everyone finds it unpleasant.

Coconut

Coconut is an important culinary ingredient in the tropics. The desiccated coconut which we are so fond of adding to cakes and biscuits is seldom used. Instead a delicious coconut milk is made by infusing fresh shredded coconut flesh in hot water and extracting the juice. It is used mainly for flavouring savoury dishes. Presumably a rather crude type of milk can be made by soaking desiccated coconut but I prefer to buy blocks of creamed coconut, dissolving it in a little hot water until the desired consistency is reached.

Coriander

Most commonly thought of as a spice it may come as a surprise to learn that fresh coriander is reputed to be the world's most commonly used

herb. It is sometimes referred to as Chinese or Japanese parsley and takes the place of parsley in the Far East, South East Asia, India, the Middle East, Mexico and Spanish America. It has an unusual but irresistible flavour and should be used liberally in dishes originating from the above-mentioned countries. Some cooks suggest using fresh European parsley if coriander is unavailable but in my opinion they are as different as chalk and cheese.

Coriander seeds are small, round and brittle and vary in colour from cream through to shades of light brown and pale green. They have a lovely sweet smell which is vaguely reminiscent of oranges and is enhanced by dry roasting. Coriander is an essential ingredient in curried dishes and vegetables à la grecque.

Cumin

A warm, sweet-smelling aromatic spice used extensively in Spanish, Mexican, Indian, North African and Middle Eastern cooking. Cumin seeds are similar in appearance to caraway, but the two can not be mistaken in the kitchen for they smell completely different. If ground cumin is required it is better to buy whole cumin seeds and to grind them at home, after dry roasting in a frying pan for a few minutes to bring out their full flavour.

Curry Powder

Curry powder is rarely, if ever, used in authentic eastern dishes. It is a European invention, intended to simplify the task of making a curry. A typical curry powder is made up of four parts red pepper, three parts turmeric, one part white pepper, one part cloves and a little nutmeg. There is no reason today why every kitchen should not contain at least the basic curry spices for they are all reasonably cheap and readily available. However, I must own up to the fact that my spice rack does hold a small pot of medium curry powder which I use, as a last minute seasoning, to 'pep up' English as well as eastern dishes.

Dill
The name is derived from the old Norse word 'dilla' meaning to lull, and certainly dill water is said to have a soothing influence on young children. It is still a popular herb in Scandanavian countries but more for its culinary properties. Dill is a standard flavouring for fish, potatoes and pickled cucumbers. Both the seeds and feathery green leaves (dill weed) are used. Dill weed does not dry satisfactorily and should be quick-frozen instead.

Fennel
Fennel has fine feathery green leaves and small oval seeds which smell sweetly of aniseed. It is known as the 'fish herb' and is most popular in Mediterranean countries where it grows wild in fields and on roadsides. Do not confuse the fennel herb with the bulbous Florence fennel sold in many vegetable shops. Although members of the same family their culinary use is different.

Fenugreek
Angular, mustard coloured seeds which are slightly bitter in taste. To bring out the true flavour of fenugreek dry roast before grinding to a powder. Do not roast for too long or the seeds become horribly bitter. Fenugreek is added to

most commercial curry powders. Use with discretion.

Garam Masala
Garam masala is a mixture of aromatic spices used to give a little panache to curried dishes. There is no standard recipe but it should include cardamom, cinnamon, black cumin seeds, cloves, black peppercorns and nutmeg. I buy it ready-made, storing it in small, air-tight containers. Use garam masala sparingly and add it to a dish as a final seasoning, just before serving.

Garlic
It is difficult to describe the flavour of garlic for although a member of the onion family it has a very different smell and taste. It is one of those tantalising ingredients which, when used in moderation, is noticed more by its effect on the overall taste than by its dominance. How much garlic to add to a dish depends entirely upon personal taste. One of the main reasons people

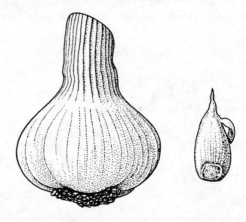

give for not using it is the fear of being offensive to others. Dumas summed up the situation perfectly when he wrote 'everyone recognises the smell of garlic, except the person who has eaten it and who has no idea why everyone hurries away when he approaches'.* In fact, I find that modest amounts of garlic are hardly detectable but to be doubly sure one can always eat a little fresh parsley or drink some red wine, both of which are reputed to counteract garlicky odours and leave the breath smelling fresh and sweet.

Ginger

Ginger is another indispensible flavouring. Most cooks have a small pot of ground ginger for adding to biscuits, cakes, puddings and desserts. I prefer fresh root ginger, particularly for savoury dishes, and keep a little in the refrigerator where it will stay good for up to three weeks. To use it, simply peel and grate finely. Don't add it to very hot fat as it will quickly burn and become bitter. The taste of fresh root ginger is milder, subtler and more aromatic than that of dried ginger root or powdered ginger. Dried root ginger is hard and shrivelled-looking and must be bruised, that is to say broken open, to release the flavour.

Herbs

The use of herbs has declined to such an extent that few modern gardens contain anything more than a small patch of mint or parsley. Nonetheless there is no reason why fresh herbs shouldn't be available to any cook all the year round. Most are much better flavoured than dried varieties and can

* A. Dumas — Dumas on Food

be used both as a seasoning and as a garnish. Herbs grow well in pots and window boxes and are ideal plants for small gardens. If you have difficulty obtaining the herbs needed for my recipes do use dried ones, but remember that their flavour is much stronger and one teaspoon of dried herb is the equivalent to one tablespoon of fresh herb.

Lemon

I use lemon juice in all types of cooking, from hearty stews to stir-fried vegetables and salads. It is a souring agent par excellence, adding piquancy without affecting the flavour or texture of a dish. I sometimes wonder whether I perhaps use lemon juice where others use salt! To obtain a true lemon flavour it is necessary to use the grated rind or zest for the essential oils are to be found in the skin rather than in the juice.

Limes

Limes resemble small green lemons. They are an important flavouring in the cooking of many tropical countries but unfortunately are not always readily available in colder climates and can be expensive. Lime juice is sharper and more aromatic than lemon juice. It is best to wait until limes are in season before trying out recipes calling for them. Lemon juice is no substitute.

Mace

Two spices, nutmeg and mace, are to be found on the nutmeg tree. The fruits of the tree are like ochre-coloured plums and when ripe they split open to reveal the brilliant red mace which forms a cage around the glossy brown shell of the nutmeg. Occasionally it is possible to buy nutmeg still clasped in the finger-like grip of the mace, but more commonly the two spices are sold separately. Mace fades to an orangy-yellow colour as it dries. It is much more expensive than the humbler nutmeg and has a delicate, finer flavour. It is used to flavour sauces, potted meats, sausages and fish as well as sweet spiced cakes and biscuits.

Marjoram
Sweet marjoram is a herb with a delicate flavour similar to that of oregano. It can be used with meat, fowl and game and in vegetable and salad dishes, especially with tomatoes. The flavour is easily masked by strong-tasting foods and is destroyed by lengthy cooking. I recommend that whenever possible marjoram is added at the last moment.

Mint
Surely one of the most popular garden herbs, mint is best known as an accompaniment to roast lamb, although the French think this barbaric. It is also an essential ingredient when boiling new potatoes. It should always be used fresh, the dried product having a very poor flavour.

Miso
A Japanese flavouring made of soya beans and cereal grains, fermented with water and salt. Strictly speaking I should not be including it in a low-salt book because it contains quite a large amount of salt. It is an interesting and unusual seasoning which can be enjoyed once in a while. However I would not recommend it to those following a strict low-sodium diet. There are three basic types of miso — mugi miso, genmai miso and hatcho miso. I prefer mugi miso, finding it more versatile than genmai miso which is a little too sweet for my palate. I find hatcho miso a little too strong in flavour. The consistency of miso is that of a stiff paste and generally it is thinned down with a little stock or water before being stirred into soups, stews, sauces etc. Whenever possible add it at the very last minute, just before serving, because much of its goodness is destroyed by heat.

Mustard
There are three basic types of mustard seeds:
1. small black/brown seeds which are used whole in many curried foods. They are not especially hot and have a deliciously nutty flavour.
2. larger black mustard seeds which are very hot and spicy and are most commonly ground to a paste.
3. white or yellow mustard seeds which are less hot than the large black ones and can be used whole in pickles or ground into mustard powder.

Occasionally I will use a ready-made mustard paste. I prefer Dijon mustard which is light in colour, clean tasting and moderately hot. English mustards are much, much hotter. Most ready-made mustards contain added salt, and those on a strict low-sodium diet should make their own mustard. The recipe is given on page 107.

Nutmeg
A lovely, sweet, warming spice which is best bought whole and grated when needed. In Britain

nutmeg is traditionally thought of as a flavouring for cakes, puddings and mulled wines but it also has a special affinity with meat, cheese and spinach. The Italians are particularly fond of it and grate a little into sauces and over Mozzarella cheese. It is popular in India where it is an essential ingredient in garam masala, and in the Middle East.

Oils

One's choice of cooking oils is very important and I recommend that you buy more than one type. For Mediterranean-style meals use a full-bodied olive oil, Chinese dishes are best cooked in peanut or soya oil, and Indian curries should be made with ghee (clarified butter) or sesame oil. Corn oil, on the other hand, makes deliciously nutty pastries, sunflower oil is a good all-rounder and walnut oil makes a superb salad dressing.

Oregano

Oregano is a very popular herb in Italy where it is added to almost every conceivable type of dish. It needs hot, humid conditions and some of the very best oregano comes from southern Italy. Botanically speaking wild marjoram, which grows in cooler temperate climates, is a form of oregano but without the hot sunshine to bring out the full flavour it is something of a pallid and uninteresting herb and cannot be compared with its full-blooded cousin.

Parsley

Little needs to be said about the ubiquitous parsley plant. It can be used as little or as often as you like for its refreshing flavour goes with most foods.

Pepper

Ready-ground pepper tastes dusty and flat compared with that freshly-ground from a pepper mill. I always use black peppercorns as I prefer their flavour, but white ones are supposed to be better for creamy soups and sauces, purely because of their colour, as they do not spoil the clean appearance of white foods. Other useful peppers are:

Cayenne — a particular type of ground red chilli pepper, thought to have originated from Cayenne in French Guyana. There is usually little difference between cayenne and chilli powder.

Chilli — fresh chilli peppers vary in size, colour and strength and should be used with extreme caution except by hardened chilli eaters (notably the Mexicans and Indians). The seeds are much hotter than the fleshy part and are often discarded by western cooks. When buying fresh chillies always select those which look fresh, bright, glossy and firm. Chillies contain irritants which can actually 'burn' and raise blisters on the skin. Wash your hands as soon as you have finished chopping them and refrain from touching your eyes or mouth. I rarely use dried chillies, preferring to use

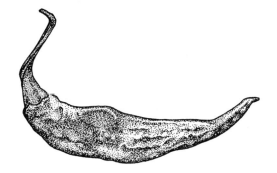

either fresh chillies or red chilli powder.

Paprika — paprika is faintly hot but is used more for its sweet aromatic flavour. It is brick red in colour and is generally associated with the national cuisine of Hungary. Indeed Hungarian paprika is of the best quality and should be bought in preference to inferior grades. Paprika is the essential flavouring in goulash and chicken paprika.

Rosemary

Rosemary is one of my favourite herbs and I use it, especially in the winter, to flavour hotpots, casseroles, sautéed potatoes and bean pies. It has a strong, robust flavour and a smell reminiscent of ginger. It should be used with discretion — a little goes a long way. It is now fashionable to flavour lamb with rosemary.

Saffron

Saffron comes from the pistils of a lavender-blue crocus and it has been estimated that five thousand flowers are needed to produce one ounce of fresh saffron. It is little wonder that it is so expensive. Turmeric and marigold petals are cheaper and colour foods yellow but they do not have the subtle flavour of saffron and cannot be used in such dishes as bouillabaise, saffron bread and saffron sauces. Always buy the whole, brilliant vermillion, saffron pistils. To use, crush half a dozen and leave to soak in a tablespoon or two of hot stock or water until the liquid has taken on a bright orange hue. Strain and add the liquid to the other ingredients. When cooking a stew or soup I do not bother to soak the saffron first but throw it straight into the pot.

Savory

A neglected herb and one not held in very high regard by most cooks although I think it has quite a pleasant flavour, rather like thyme, and I use it quite often in rissoles, stews, pies etc.

Sesame Seeds

Sesame seeds are used mainly as a garnish, sprinkled on breads, cakes and biscuits. They have a slightly nutty taste which is greatly enhanced by dry roasting. More important, however, than the seeds themselves is the creamy paste, known as tahini, which is made by grinding them. I use it as the basis for many salad dressings, bean purées and vegetable dips and instead of an egg to bind burger and rissole mixtures. Dark tahini is ground from unhulled sesame seeds and has a stronger flavour than white or light tahini.

Sour Cream

Sourness is a pure taste sensation which seems to become even more important to the palate as the amount of salt consumed drops. I often find myself adding a little lemon juice, wine, wine vinegar, yoghurt or sour cream to a dish as the final adjustment before taking it to the table. Sour cream is very popular in Eastern Europe and Russia. It is richer than yoghurt and sharper than double cream. Sour cream, like all dairy products, is high in saturated fat and sodium and should be used sparingly.

Soya Sauce

Soya sauce is a common seasoning agent in the Far East and is becoming increasingly popular in the West too. It is made from fermented soya beans, wheat flour, water and salt and is similar in flavour to miso. It is very easy to become totally reliant on soya sauce with the result that everything from the nut cutlets to the shepherd's pie tastes exactly the same. Continual heavy use of soya sauce is said to be bad for the liver to say nothing of the effect the high salt content has upon one's blood pressure. Discounting those made artificially from monosodium glutamate, caramel, sugar and water, there are two grades of natural soya sauce, tamari and shoyu. Tamari is richer and thicker than shoyu and is consequently more expensive. However, it is used in much smaller quantities, one teaspoon of tamari being equivalent in strength to two teaspoons of shoyu. Despite its high salt content I believe that it is so valuable to the cook that its occasional, restrained use is justified for those not following a low-sodium diet.

Tarragon
Tarragon is a fragrant herb which is traditionally used to flavour fish, chicken and sauce tartare.

Thyme
Thyme is my favourite herb. Its smell and pretty mauve flowers remind me of cycling holidays in Provence when I pick wild thyme at the roadside to brighten up my camp meals. It is suitable for almost every conceivable dish. I sprinkle it over lightly-cooked vegetables, especially carrots, peppers and courgettes (zucchini) and use it in rissole mixtures. The attractively variegated lemon thyme makes excellent stuffings for fish.

Tomatoes
Tomatoes are indispensible, available all year round (at a price), brightly coloured, richly flavoured and versatile. Who could ask for more? — but please try to restrain your enthusiasm. Adding a tablespoon of tomato purée or several chopped tomatoes will give colour and depth of flavour but there are many other equally interesting ways of enlivening a dish. 'Happy', says one writer, 'is the cook who knows how to use the tomato with discretion'.*

Turmeric
Turmeric has a peculiar earthy flavour and is a deep yellow ochre colour. Always use it in Indian recipes rather than saffron which is wasted in curries. It is a useful spice giving mustard, pickles and curries their characteristic colour.

Vinegar
It gives added flavour to certain dishes and counteracts excessive richness. Vinegars used in the modern kitchen have become much smoother than the rasping malt vinegar the British love to sprinkle over chipped potatoes. I use a good wine vinegar, both red and white, finding cider vinegar a little too reminiscent of scrumpy. A good, well-flavoured vinegar is particularly important in salad dressings and sauces.

Wine
I rarely have half empty bottles of wine in the house (or full ones come to that) but I do enjoy adding a dash of wine to my cooking. I buy half or quarter bottles of reasonably good quality wine specifically for the kitchen. Once opened wine

* Elizabeth David — 'French Provincial Cooking'

soon become sour but it will stay in good
condition, for a time, if stored in air-tight
containers. Either transfer the wine to progressively
smaller bottles as you use it or freeze in an ice tray
and drop a cube or two into the stew, casserole
etc. as and when needed.

Yoghurt
Another sour milk product which adds piquancy
and flavour to many dishes. It is used extensively
as a marinade for meat, in soups and salad
dressings and in cooked dishes. Yoghurt can be
gently heated in sauces and can be stirred into hot
dishes as a final seasoning, but when cooked in a
dish it will separate out. The addition of an egg or
a tablespoon or two of flour will prevent this from
happening.

Recipes

The recipes in the book are primarily intended to be free from added salt but some do include foods which contain moderate to high amounts of sodium. Salt-free cooking need not mean limiting oneself to boring and unappetising dishes or sacrificing one's enjoyment of good food for the sake of one's health. Eating should be a pleasure and I am not averse to including a little cheese, eggs, milk, meat, fish or even a dash of soya sauce in some of my recipes. There is a world of difference between eating the occasional stir-fry or 'au gratin' dish and constantly smothering one's food with table salt. Those readers who, for medical reasons, must follow a low-sodium diet will find many delicious and suitable recipes in the book. I would, however, suggest that they check the ingredients against their list of permitted foodstuffs.

An important principle to remember when cooking without salt is that as the flavour is not being 'enhanced' or disguised by salt the quality of the ingredients is of prime importance. With careful buying and seasoning there should be no reason why anyone should notice the absence of salt and even less reason for using expensive salt substitutes which seem to be flooding onto the market these days.

Soups

Cream of Watercress Soup

Metric/Imperial	American
1 mild onion	1 mild onion
1 clove garlic	1 clove garlic
350 g/12 oz potatoes	¾ lb potatoes
2 bunches watercress	2 bunches watercress
25 g/1 oz unsalted butter	2-3 tbsps sweet butter
15 ml/1 tbsp sunflower oil	1½ tbsps sunflower oil
1.2 litres/2 pints chicken stock	5 cups chicken stock
1 bay leaf	1 bay leaf
freshly ground black pepper	freshly ground black pepper
freshly grated nutmeg	freshly grated nutmeg
30 ml/2 tbsps natural yoghurt	2-3 tbsps unflavored yogurt

Wash, trim and chop the vegetables. Heat the butter and oil in a pan and add the onion and garlic. Sauté for 10-15 minutes until soft. Add the potatoes and stir well. Cover with wetted greaseproof paper and a tight fitting lid. Cook for 10-15 minutes. Remove the paper and add the stock, watercress and bay leaf. Bring to the boil and simmer gently until the potatoes are soft. Remove the bay leaf. Ladle into a liquidiser and blend until smooth. Season with black pepper and nutmeg.

Stir in the yoghurt and garnish with a sprig of watercress.

Serve with a dish of freshly made wholewheat croûtons.

Potage Bonne Femme

Metric/Imperial
5 leeks
4 medium potatoes
25 g/1 oz unsalted butter
15 ml/1 tbsp sunflower oil
425 ml/15 fl oz milk
425 ml/15 fl oz water
30-45 ml/2-3 tbsps fresh
  parsley, chopped
10 ml/2 level tsps English
  mustard
freshly ground black pepper

American
5 leeks
4 medium potatoes
2-3 tbsps sweet butter
1½ tbsp sunflower oil
1¾ cups milk
1¾ cups water
3-4 tbsps fresh parsley,
  chopped
2 tsps English mustard
freshly ground black pepper

Wash, trim and chop the leeks and potatoes. Melt the butter and oil in a large pan and add the vegetables. Sauté lightly for 5-10 minutes. Cover with wetted greaseproof paper and a tight fitting lid. Cook over a low heat for 10 minutes. Remove the greaseproof paper and pour in the milk and water. Bring to the boil, stirring frequently. Replace the pan lid and simmer gently for 15 minutes.

Pass through a vegetable mouli or blend until smooth and creamy. Return to the pan and stir in the parsley and mustard. Heat through and season to taste with black pepper.

Serve with wholewheat soda bread.

Fresh Tomato Soup

Metric/Imperial
2 onions
1 clove garlic
25 g/1 oz unsalted butter
30 ml/2 tbsp olive oil
675 g/1½ lbs tomatoes
75 g/3 oz ground almonds
575 ml/1 pint water
5-10 ml/1 -2 level tsps
  dried basil
5 ml/1 tsp lemon juice
  (optional)
freshly ground black pepper

American
2 onions
1 clove garlic
2-3 tbsps sweet butter
2-3 tbsps olive oil
1½ lbs tomatoes
¾ cup ground almonds
2½ cups water
1-2 tsps dried basil
1 tsp lemon juice (optional)
freshly ground black pepper

Peel and chop the onion and garlic. Heat the butter and oil in a pan and sauté the vegetables until soft. Chop the tomatoes and add to the pan. Cook for 5 minutes, stirring frequently. Blend the ground almonds and water together and pour over the tomatoes. Bring to the boil and simmer for 15-20 minutes.

Pass the ingredients through a vegetable mouli or blend until smooth and creamy. Add the basil and lemon juice and season with black pepper. Heat through before serving.

Pumpkins

The golden-coloured pumpkin is appreciated more by those making Halloween lanterns than it is by the cook. Classed on a par with the green marrow it is widely assumed to be bland, watery and unappetising. This does the pumpkin a grave injustice for although it is not in the same league as the courgette or zucchini it is far superior in flavour, texture and colour to the marrow. The culinary merits of the pumpkin are best displayed in America, where it is used in breads, soups and a delicious, spiced pie traditionally eaten to celebrate Thanksgiving.

Pumpkin Soup with Yoghurt

Metric/Imperial	American
450 g/1 lb pumpkin	1 lb pumpkin
225 g/8 oz carrots	½ lb carrots
850 ml/1½ pints water	3¼ cups water
1 onion	1 onion
25 g/1 oz unsalted butter	2-3 tbsps sweet butter
15 ml/1 tbsp sunflower oil	1½ tbsps sunflower oil
225 g/8 oz tomatoes	½ lb tomatoes
10 ml/2 tsps dried basil	2 tsps dried basil
freshly ground black pepper	freshly ground black pepper
150 ml/5 fl oz natural yoghurt	½ cup unflavored yogurt

Peel, de-seed and chop the pumpkin. Wash, trim and slice the carrots. Place the vegetables in a large pan with the water. Bring to the boil. Simmer for 20 minutes until the vegetables are tender. Drain and reserve the cooking water.

Peel and chop finely the onion. Sauté in the butter and oil until soft. Chop coarsely the tomatoes and mix with the onions. Cook for a further 5 minutes. Put the pumpkin, onion and tomato mixture and 275 ml/10 fl oz (1¼ cups) of cooking water into a liquidiser. Blend until smooth and creamy. Return to the pan. Season to taste with basil and black pepper. Heat thoroughly.

Pour into serving bowls and swirl a little yoghurt in each before serving.

Carrot and Coriander Soup

Metric/Imperial	American
450 g/1 lb carrots	1 lb carrots
450 g/1 lb potatoes	1 lb potatoes
1.6 litres/2¾ pints water	6¾ cups water
2 onions	2 onions
25 g/1 oz unsalted butter	2-3 tbsps sweet butter
30 ml/2 tbsps corn oil	2-3 tbsps corn oil
20-25 ml/4-5 tsps ground coriander	4-5 tsps ground coriander
30 ml/2 tbsps wholewheat flour	2-3 tbsps wholewheat flour
10 ml/2 tsps lemon juice	2 tsps lemon juice
30-45 ml/2-3 tbsps fresh coriander, chopped	3-4 tbsps fresh coriander, chopped
freshly ground black pepper	freshly ground black pepper

Wash, trim and chop the carrots and potatoes. Place in a pan with the water and bring to the boil. Cook until soft. Drain and reserve the vegetable stock. Pass the cooked vegetables through a vegetable mouli or sieve.

Peel and finely chop the onions. Heat the butter and oil in a frying pan and lightly sauté the onions until soft and golden brown. Stir in the ground coriander and fry for 2-3 minutes. Stir in the flour and cook for a further minute or two. Gradually add the vegetable stock, lemon juice and puréed vegetables.

Heat through before serving and season with fresh coriander and black pepper.

Carrot and Cashew Nut Soup

Metric/Imperial	American
175 g/6 oz cashew nuts	1¼ cups cashew nuts
350 g/12 oz carrots	¾ lb carrots
2 medium parsnips	2 medium parsnips
2 medium onions	2 medium onions
15 g/½ oz unsalted butter	1½ tbsps sweet butter
15 ml/1 tbsp sunflower oil	1½ tbsps sunflower oil
freshly ground black pepper	freshly ground black pepper

Grind the nuts in a blender. Leave them in the goblet.

Clean and slice the carrots and parsnips. Cook in boiling water for 8-10 minutes. Drain and reserve the cooking water. Add sufficient water to make 850 ml/1½ pints (3¼ cups) vegetable stock. Peel and chop the onions. Heat the butter and oil in a frying pan and sauté the onions until soft. Place the cooked vegetables and stock in the blender with the nuts. Blend until smooth and creamy. Rub the soup through a sieve and reheat in a saucepan. Season with black pepper.

Serve with wholewheat croûtons.

Chestnuts

Whilst in Trafalgar Square one cold December day several years ago I was delighted to see a street vendor roasting chestnuts over a brazier. I, and many other people, took the opportunity to sample his wares and warm our hands.

The venture must have proved both popular and successful for it is now possible once again to buy freshly roasted chestnuts in many towns. In some cases the open brazier has been replaced by a machine resembling a small traction engine and the damp, chilly streets are sometimes forsaken in favour of warm and brightly lit shopping malls. Although the modern chestnut vendor isn't quite as evocative as the Dickensian street scene I experienced in London the chestnuts certainly taste as good.

There are however many other ways of eating chestnuts — from the traditional chestnut stuffing served with the Christmas dinner to the exotic 'marrons glacés'. To discover the real delights of these mahogany coloured and rich-tasting nuts we must study the cuisine of European countries. For example, in Italy they are an essential ingredient in 'castagnaccio', a dish made with chestnut flour, sultanas, pine kernels and fennel seeds; the French use them in 'soufflé aux marrons et potiron' (chestnut and pumpkin soufflé), from Spain comes 'castañas con mantequilla' (braised celery and chestnut served with butter sauce) and from Austria the delicious Nesselrode pudding or chestnut ice.

Having sampled many chestnut recipes I must admit to being something of an enthusiast. However, as well as praising the chestnut's culinary delights I feel it my duty to point out its principal disadvantage — it is both awkward and time consuming to prepare. The hard outer shell and the brown, wrinkled inner skin must be removed.

In an effort to make life easier I have experimented with dried, shelled chestnuts which can be bought throughout the year in many shops. Unfortunately their poor texture and flavour do not make up for the time and effort saved in their preparation.

When buying fresh chestnuts select the largest you can find, for although they may be a little more expensive they are quicker to peel than the smaller ones. There are several methods of preparing chestnuts — they can be roasted in front of an open fire, baked in the oven or cooked in boiling water. I use the latter method. First make a cut with a sharp knife in the outer shell of each nut. Put them in a pan of cold water and bring to the boil. Simmer gently for 20 minutes and then immerse in cold water. Take them out of the water one at a time and remove the outer and inner shells. If the inner skins are particularly stubborn try frying the shelled chestnuts in a little butter or oil. The inner skin soon becomes crisp and brittle and can be rubbed off by rolling the nuts in a cloth.

If their preparation sounds arduous let me give you a word of encouragement — the effort is always worthwhile for in my view fresh chestnuts are one of the most versatile and delicious of foods.

Chestnut Soup

Metric/Imperial	American
450 g/1 lb chestnuts	1 lb chestnuts
1 stick celery	1 stick celery
1 carrot	1 carrot
1 clove garlic	1 clove garlic
1 onion	1 onion
30 ml/2 tbsps olive oil	2-3 tbsps olive oil
425 ml/15 fl oz water	1¾ cups water
275 ml/10 fl oz milk	1¼ cups milk
freshly ground black pepper	freshly ground black pepper
30 ml/2 tbsps fresh lemon thyme, chopped	2-3 tbsps fresh lemon thyme, chopped

Peel and prepare the chestnuts as directed above. Chop coarsely.

Wash, trim and chop the vegetables. Heat the oil in a large pan and sauté the vegetables for 8-10 minutes. Add the water and cook gently until soft. Place in a liquidiser with the milk and chopped chestnuts. Blend until smooth and creamy. Heat through and season with black pepper. Ladle into serving bowls and sprinkle with lemon thyme.

Serve with a crusty loaf.

Soupe au Pistou

Looking through the ingredients for this soup you might well think that 'Soupe au Pistou' is simply a rather grand name for that old perennial 'minestrone'. Although the two soups are similar in many ways there is one essential ingredient which puts this soup in a class of its own. That is 'pistou', a delicious creamy sauce made from pounded pine nuts, garlic, basil and olive oil which is commonly eaten with soups and pastas.

Metric/Imperial	American
100 g/4 oz dried haricot beans, soaked and drained	½ cup navy beans, soaked and drained
275 g/10 fl oz water	1¼ cups water
1 bay leaf	1 bay leaf
1 yellow pepper	1 yellow pepper
1 leek	1 leek
1 onion	1 onion
100 g/4 oz French beans	¼ lb snap beans
1 courgette	1 zucchini
450 g/1 lb tomatoes, peeled	1 lb tomatoes, peeled
30 ml/2 tbsps olive oil	2-3 tbsps olive oil
1.2 litres/2 pints vegetable/ bean stock	5 cups vegetable/bean stock
50 g/2 oz wholewheat macaroni	½ cup wholewheat macaroni
freshly ground black pepper	freshly ground black pepper

For the pistou	For the pistou
3 cloves garlic	3 cloves garlic
12 sprigs of fresh basil	12 sprigs of fresh basil
25 g/1 oz pine kernels	1 tbsp pine kernels (pignoli)
45-60 ml/3-4 tbsps olive oil	4-5 tbsps olive oil

Place the haricot beans in a pan or pressure cooker with the water and bay leaf. Simmer for 45-50 minutes or pressure cook at high pressure for 12 minutes. When the beans are tender, drain and reserve the stock. Discard the bay leaf.

Wash, trim and slice the vegetables. Heat the olive oil in a large pan and sauté the onion, leek and pepper for 10 minutes. Add the remaining vegetables and cook for a further 4-5 minutes. Stir in the cooked haricot beans, the stock and pasta. Bring to the boil and simmer for 15-20 minutes until the pasta is al dente. Season with black pepper.

To make the pistou, peel and chop the garlic and trim the basil. Place both ingredients with the pine kernels in a mortar and pound well. Add the oil, a little at a time, to form a smooth, creamy paste. Spoon a little pistou into the bottom of each bowl and ladle over the hot soup.

Serve with crusty bread.

Chick Pea Soup (Potaje de Garbanzos)

Metric/Imperial	American
15-30 ml/1-2 tbsps olive oil	1½-3 tbsps olive oil
4 tomatoes, chopped	4 tomatoes, chopped
2 onions, sliced	2 onions, sliced
2 cloves garlic, peeled and crushed	2 cloves garlic, peeled and crushed
225 g/8 oz chick peas, soaked overnight	1 cup chick peas, soaked overnight
850 ml/1½ pints water	3¼ cups water
15 ml/1 tbsp fresh parsley, chopped	1½ tbsps fresh parsley, chopped
1 bay leaf	1 bay leaf
5 ml/1 tsp paprika	1 tsp paprika
5 ml/1 tsp allspice	1 tsp allspice
15 ml/1 tbsp medium curry powder	1½ tbsps medium curry powder

To garnish:	To garnish
15 ml/1 tbsp fresh parsley, chopped	1½ tbsps fresh parsley, chopped
wholewheat croûtons	wholewheat croûtons

Heat the olive oil in a large pan and sauté the tomatoes, onions and garlic for 5-10 minutes. Add the remaining ingredients and bring to the boil. Simmer for 1-1½ hours until the chick peas are soft. (Pressure cook for 20-25 minutes). Place three-quarters of the soup in a liquidiser and blend until smooth. Stir into the remaining soup. Heat through. Float the croûtons on top of the soup and sprinkle with parsley.

Serve.

Lentil Soup

Metric/Imperial	American
2 onions	2 onions
2 carrots	2 carrots
1 leek	1 leek
15 ml/1 tbsp sunflower oil	1½ tbsps sunflower oil
225 g/8 oz brown lentils	1 cup brown lentils
1 bay leaf	1 bay leaf
5 ml/1 tsp English mustard	1 tsp English mustard
1½ litres/3 pints water	6½ cups water

Brown lentils are one of my favourite pulses but they are something of a nuisance to prepare. They first have to be sorted and checked over carefully to remove all the tiny stones and pieces of grit lurking in their midst. Unfortunately the stones are invariably the same colour and size as the lentils themselves making the task all the more laborious. Don't be tempted, as I have been in the past, to assume that the beans are clean — they never are and no soup is enhanced by the crunchy texture of gravel!

Wash, trim and slice the vegetables. Heat the oil in a frying pan and sauté the vegetables for 10 minutes. Place all the ingredients in a large pan or pressure cooker and cook for 1 hour or 12 minutes respectively. Remove the bay leaf and pass the soup through a vegetable mouli or sieve. Season liberally with black pepper. Adjust consistency if necessary.

Serve with brown bread rolls for a substantial meal.

Spicy Pea and Onion Soup

Metric/Imperial

4 large onions
45 ml/3 tbsps sunflower oil
5-10 ml/1-2 tsps turmeric
a good pinch chilli powder
225 g/8 oz yellow split
   peas
1.2 litres/2 pints water
5 ml/1 tsp garam masala
fresh coriander, chopped

American

4 large onions
3-4 tbsps sunflower oil
1-2 tsps turmeric
a good pinch chili powder
1 cup yellow split peas
5 cups water
1 tsp garam masala
fresh coriander, chopped

Chop the onions. Heat the oil in a large pan and sauté the onions for 15-20 minutes until soft. Stir in the turmeric and chilli powder. Fry for 2-3 minutes. Add the split peas and water. Bring to the boil and simmer until the peas are soft. Liquidise or rub through a sieve. Add extra water if necessary. Stir in the garam masala and sprinkle with the coriander before serving.

Vegetables and Salads

VEGETABLES

Although the situation is improving there is still little respect for vegetables. This is shown not only in the all too common practice of serving frozen varieties throughout the year but also in the indiscriminate use of salt when cooking and serving all manner of vegetable dishes.

Why salt needs to be added isn't always made clear but I am sure its advocates will argue that it improves and enhances the flavour. Little wonder that they think that the flavour of most vegetables needs improving when the majority of people still cook them until they are soft and tasteless. I can only assume that they have never sampled the delights of fresh, young, tender, sweet tasting vegetables and that they see all vegetables as an accompaniment to 'the main dish'. Being mere side dishes, of course, vegetables deserve little thought, time or care in preparation and are eaten for reasons of convention and perhaps health, rather than pleasure.

It would be far better, for the sake of flavour and wholesomeness, to dispose of the salt cellar and to pay a little more attention to the quality of the vegetables and to their cooking.

Braised Green Peas with Butter

Metric/Imperial	American
1 small, crisp lettuce heart	1 small, crisp lettuce heart
450 g/1 lb small, tender peas	1 lb small, tender peas
4 shallots, sliced	4 shallots, sliced
6 sprigs parsley, tied together	6 sprigs parsley, tied together
25 g/1 oz unsalted butter	2-3 tbsps sweet butter
30 ml/2 tbsps water	2-3 tbsps water
freshly ground black pepper	freshly ground black pepper

Cut the lettuce heart into quarters and bind each segment with soft string. Place all the ingredients in a pan and bring to the boil. Toss lightly before covering. Simmer gently for 20 minutes, stirring occasionally, until the vegetables are tender. If necessary cook over a fierce heat, shaking the pan constantly, to drive off any excess water.

Remove the parsley and cut the string from the lettuce. Season to taste with black pepper. Toss before serving.

Creamed Leeks

Metric/Imperial	American
450 g/1 lb leeks, trimmed	1 lb leeks, trimmed
15 ml/1 tbsp olive oil	1½ tbsps olive oil
5 ml/1 tsp lemon juice	1 tsp lemon juice
1.25 ml/¼ tsp Dijon mustard	¼ tsp Dijon mustard
30 ml/2 tbsps sour cream	2-3 tbsps sour cream
freshly ground black pepper	freshly ground black pepper

Steam the leeks whole, or halved if very long, until barely tender. Place in a serving dish. Blend the remaining ingredients together and pour over the hot leeks. Leave to cool.

Broccoli with Thai Sauce

Metric/Imperial	American
450 g/1 lb broccoli	1 lb broccoli
150 ml/5 fl oz water	½ cup water
100 g/4 oz creamed coconut, grated	¼ lb creamed coconut, grated
2.5 ml/½ tsp turmeric	½ tsp turmeric
2.5 ml/½ tsp green cardamom seeds	½ tsp green cardamom seeds
1 bay leaf	1 bay leaf
5-10 ml/1-2 tsps lemon juice	1-2 tsps lemon juice
pinch chilli powder	pinch chili powder

Wash, trim and steam the broccoli until tender. Place all the remaining ingredients in a small pan and bring to the boil. Cook gently for a few minutes and then pour through a fine sieve. Place the broccoli in a serving dish and pour over the sauce.

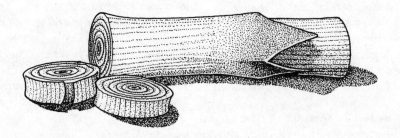

Carrots and Thyme

Wash 450 g/1 lb carrots and cut into julienne strips. Steam until tender. Sprinkle liberally with finely chopped fresh thyme and toss before serving.

Stuffed Onions

Using one sound onion per person, wash and remove the root, leaving the skin intact. Bake in a preheated oven, gas mark 4 (350°F/180°C) for one hour. When tender scoop out the centre of each onion and chop finely. Place in a small bowl and mix with a little butter, grated cheese, chopped sage and black pepper. Stuff into the onions and bake for a further 5-10 minutes.

Finely chopped walnuts or tomatoes could be used instead of the cheese.

Breaded Sprouts

Trim 450 g/1 lb brussels sprouts and steam until tender. Melt 30-45 ml/2-3 tbsps unsalted butter in a small pan. Add the same amount of soft wholewheat breadcrumbs and cook until golden brown. Season with a pinch of dried marjoram and black pepper.

Place the sprouts in a serving dish, and sprinkle the breadcrumb mixture over the top.

Stir-Fried Vegetable Medley

Metric/Imperial	American
100 g/4 oz French beans, sliced	1 cup sliced snap beans
15 ml/1 tbsp olive oil	1½ tbsps olive oil
100 g/4 oz courgettes, sliced	¼ lb zucchini, sliced
50 g/2 oz button mushrooms, halved	½ cup halved button mushrooms
15 ml/1 tbsp fresh rosemary, chopped	1½ tbsps fresh rosemary, chopped
15 ml/1 tbsp lemon juice	1½ tbsps lemon juice
freshly ground black pepper	freshly ground black pepper

Put the beans in a pan of water and boil briskly for 3-4 minutes. Drain well.

Heat the oil in a wok until very hot but not smoking. Toss in the beans and courgettes and stir-fry for 3-4 minutes. Add the mushrooms and cook for a further minute or two. Sprinkle with rosemary and lemon juice and season with black pepper. Toss well before serving.

Potatoes en Papillotes

Clean some very small new potatoes. Put them in a large piece of greaseproof paper with a sprig of thyme, a sprig of mint and a knob of unsalted butter. Fold the paper so that the potatoes are completely sealed inside. Place in a preheated oven, gas mark 5 (375°F/190°C) and cook for 40-50 minutes until tender.

Stir-Fried Mange-Tout Peas

Metric/Imperial	American
225 g/8 oz mange-tout peas	½ lb mange-tout peas
15 ml/1 tbsp sesame oil	1½ tbsps sesame oil
1 crisp lettuce heart, shredded	1 crisp lettuce heart, shredded
5 ml/1 tbsp fresh chives, chopped	1½ tbsps fresh chives, chopped

Trim the mange-touts and cook in a pan of boiling water for 2-3 minutes. Drain well.

Heat the oil in a wok and toss in the peas and lettuce. Stir-fry for 3-4 minutes. Sprinkle with chives and serve immediately.

Baked Vegetables à la Provençale

Metric/Imperial	American
2 large potatoes	2 large potatoes
2 ripe tomatoes	2 ripe tomatoes
2 medium courgettes	2 medium zucchini
1 mild onion	1 mild onion
30 ml/2 tbsps fresh parsley, chopped	2-3 tbsps fresh parsley, chopped
15 ml/1 tbsp olive oil	1½ tbsps olive oil
freshly ground black pepper	freshly ground black pepper
75 g/3 oz soft whole wheat breadcrumbs	¾ cup soft wholewheat breadcrumbs
a little water	a little water

Preheat the oven to gas mark 5 (375°F/190°C).

Wash, trim and slice the vegetables and place in a bowl. Add the parsley and olive oil and mix together well. Season with black pepper. Spoon into an oiled ovenproof dish and pour over sufficient water to cover the bottom of the dish. Sprinkle with breadcrumbs and bake for 50-60 minutes until the vegetables are tender.

SALADS

Salads are generally quick and easy to prepare and can be made from almost any conceivable ingredient, from the simple bowl of salad greens to the more substantial salade composée which can contain fish, poultry, meat, cheese, eggs, beans, rice and potatoes.

The ingredients must be in prime condition, selected for their variety of colour, texture and flavour, and tossed in a complementary dressing. Some of my favourite combinations are: lettuce, cucumber, orange and hazel nuts tossed in an orange dressing; grated carrot and sliced tomato with an olive oil vinaigrette; crisp lettuce, yellow pepper, baby courgettes and grated carrot in a walnut oil dressing; and beansprouts, celery, red apples and chopped mint mixed with yoghurt.

An important aspect of salad making is the visual appearance. Choose yellow or red peppers, spring onions, green or black grapes, lemon or orange rind twists, carrots, chicory, sweetcorn, yellow courgettes for their colour combinations. Fresh herbs can also add visual interest as well as flavour to a dish. Chop them into the salad just before it is tossed. Tomatoes and basil, cucumber and mint, carrots and thyme are particularly good together.

To prepare salad greens wash them quickly but thoroughly in cold running water and discard any discoloured or wilted leaves. Drain and remove surplus moisture by shaking them gently in a lettuce basket or spinning them in a rotary salad drier. Handle them carefully to avoid unnecessary bruising. Place the whole leaves in a plastic bag and store in the refrigerator until needed. Tear into even-sized pieces and mix with the other ingredients just before tossing with the dressing.

The choice of dressing is almost as varied as the salad ingredients themselves, but as a general rule green salads are best in a light French dressing whereas salades composées go better with rich, creamier sauces. I usually use white wine vinegar or lemon juice in my dressings but cider vinegar, lime juice and orange juice are good alternatives. The choice of oil is however more important, for poor quality oil can make a salad taste very unpleasant. Sunflower oil or groundnut oil are especially suited to salads whose delicate flavours are easily masked. Being richer, olive oil is admirably suited to more robust salads and those including Mediterranean ingredients such as beefsteak tomatoes, basil, olives, courgettes, capsicums and feta or Mozzarella cheese.

My favourite salad oil is walnut oil which is rich and aromatic. Difficult to find and rather expensive but well worth the effort and cost involved, as the small amount needed for each salad costs very little when compared with the other ingredients.

Watercress and Grapefruit Salad

Metric/Imperial
1 bunch watercress
small flat lettuce
¼ cucumber
25 g/1 oz lightly roasted
   hazel nuts
1 grapefruit

American
1 bunch watercress
small flat lettuce
¼ cucumber
¼ cup lightly roasted hazel
   nuts
1 grapefruit

Trim and wash the watercress and lettuce. Dry well. Tear the lettuce leaves into bite-sized pieces and place in a bowl with the watercress. Cut the cucumber in half lengthways and slice thinly. Add to the other ingredients. Chop the nuts in half and put into the bowl. Peel the grapefruit and remove the pips and pith. Working over the bowl, carefully peel away the membrane and drop each segment into the salad. Toss lightly and serve.

For those with a slightly sweeter tooth replace the grapefruit with a large orange.

Beansprout Salad

Metric/Imperial
225 g/8 oz beansprouts
100 g/4 oz button
   mushrooms, sliced
100 g/4 oz French beans,
   sliced and cooked
60 ml/4 tbsps sunflower oil
30 ml/2 tbsps lemon juice
pinch mustard powder
30 ml/2 tbsps fresh chives,
   chopped

American
½ lb beansprouts
1 cup sliced button
   mushrooms
¼ lb snap beans, sliced and
   cooked
5-6 tbsps sunflower oil
2-3 tbsps lemon juice
pinch mustard powder
2-3 tbsps fresh chives,
   chopped

Put all the salad vegetables in a large bowl. Mix the oil and lemon juice together and season with a little mustard. Pour the dressing over the salad and toss lightly. Spoon into a serving dish and sprinkle with chives.

Serve immediately.

Layer Salad

Arrange the ingredients in a large glass salad bowl in the following order:

Metric/Imperial	American
100 g/4 oz red kidney beans, cooked	½ cup red kidney beans, cooked
½ small fennel bulb, chopped	½ small fennel bulb, chopped
1 large green pepper, chopped	1 large green pepper, chopped
1 lettuce heart, shredded	1 lettuce heart, shredded
2 large carrots, grated	2 large carrots, grated
small bunch radishes, diced	small bunch radishes, diced
2 apples, grated	2 apples, grated
50 g/2 oz chopped walnuts	½ cup chopped walnuts
10 fresh dates, chopped	10 fresh dates, chopped
1 head chicory, shredded	1 head chicory, shredded
30 ml/2 tbsps fresh parsley, chopped	2-3 tbsps fresh parsley, chopped

Serve.

Salade de Ventoux

Metric/Imperial	American
3 tomatoes	3 tomatoes
4 carrots, coarsely grated	4 carrots, coarsely grated
45 ml/3 tbsps olive oil	3-4 tbsps olive oil
15 ml/1 tbsp lemon juice	1½ tbsps lemon juice
freshly ground black pepper	freshly ground black pepper

Slice the tomatoes thickly and place in a salad bowl with the grated carrot. Blend the olive oil and lemon juice together and season with black pepper. Pour the dressing over the salad, toss and leave to marinate for 1-2 hours. Toss again before serving.

Carrot and Sultana Salad

Metric/Imperial	*American*
1 lb carrots, coarsely grated	1 lb carrots, coarsely grated
100 g/4 oz sultanas	¾ cup sultanas
150 ml/5 fl oz thick natural yoghurt	½ cup thick unflavored yogurt
15 ml/1 tbsp fresh orange juice	1½ tbsps fresh orange juice
30 ml/2 tbsps lightly roasted sunflower seeds	2-3 tbsps lightly roasted sunflower seeds

Put the carrots and sultanas in a bowl. Mix the yoghurt and orange juice together and pour over the carrots. Leave for several hours. Just before serving spoon into a salad bowl and sprinkle with sunflower seeds.

Walnut Salad

Metric/Imperial	*American*
1 head chicory, shredded	1 head chicory, shredded
1 bunch watercress, trimmed	1 bunch watercress, trimmed
1 lettuce heart, shredded	1 lettuce heart, shredded
1 yellow pepper, sliced	1 yellow pepper, sliced
small bunch radishes, sliced	small bunch radishes, sliced
75 g/3 oz walnuts, chopped	¾ cup chopped walnuts
45 ml/3 tbsp walnut oil	3-4 tbsps walnut oil
15 ml/1 tbsp lemon juice	1½ tbsps lemon juice
freshly ground black pepper	freshly ground black pepper

Place all the salad vegetables and the walnuts in a large bowl. Blend the walnut oil and lemon juice together and season with a little pepper. Pour over the salad and toss lightly. Place in a salad bowl and serve immediately.

Joseph's Technicolour Salad

Metric/Imperial	American
1 handful young spinach leaves	1 handful young spinach leaves
1 lettuce heart	1 lettuce heart
1 yellow courgette	1 yellow zucchini
1 green pepper	1 green pepper
3 tomatoes	3 tomatoes
bunch spring onions	bunch scallions
4 small carrots	4 small carrots
60 ml/4 tbsps walnut oil	5-6 tbsps walnut oil
30 ml/2 tbsps fresh orange juice	2-3 tbsps fresh orange juice
freshly ground black pepper	freshly ground black pepper

Trim, wash and dry the spinach and lettuce leaves. Tear into medium-sized pieces. Slice the courgette and green pepper. Cut the tomatoes into wedges and chop the spring onions. Coarsely grate the carrots.

Place all the salad vegetables in a large bowl. Mix the walnut oil and orange juice together and season with a little black pepper. Pour the dressing over the salad and toss lightly. Place in a salad bowl and serve immediately.

Tomato and Onion Salad

Metric/Imperial	American
4 tomatoes, sliced	4 tomatoes, sliced
1 mild onion, sliced	1 mild onion, sliced
30 ml/2 tbsps fresh parsley, chopped	2-3 tbsps fresh parsley, chopped
15 ml/1 tbsp lemon juice	1½ tbsps lemon juice
45 ml/3 tbsps olive oil	3-4 tbsps olive oil
1 clove garlic, peeled and crushed	1 clove garlic, peeled and crushed
freshly ground black pepper	freshly ground black pepper

Arrange the tomato and onion slices attractively on a serving plate. Sprinkle with parsley. Place the remaining ingredients together in a jar and shake well. Pour the dressing over the salad and serve immediately.

Mint Salad

Metric/Imperial	American
1 small lettuce, shredded	1 small lettuce, shredded
225 g/8 oz tomatoes, chopped	½ lb tomatoes, chopped
¼ cucumber, diced	¼ cucumber, diced
bunch spring onions, chopped	bunch scallions, chopped
15 ml/1 tbsp fresh mint, chopped	1½ tbsps fresh mint, chopped
45 ml/3 tbsps groundnut oil	3-4 tbsps peanut oil
15 ml/1 tbsp white wine vinegar	1½ tbsps white wine vinegar
freshly ground black pepper	freshly ground black pepper

Mix the lettuce, tomatoes, cucumber, onions and mint together in a bowl. Blend the oil and vinegar together and season with a little black pepper. Pour the dressing over the salad. Toss lightly and spoon into a salad bowl. Serve immediately.

Tabouli

Tabouli or tabbouleh is a refreshing salad from the Lebanon. The principal ingredient is a cracked wheat product known as bulgar or burghul which requires very little cooking. It is pleasantly filling without being heavy or stodgy and is ideal for hot weather.

Metric/Imperial	American
225 g/8 oz bulgar	2 cups bulgar
850 ml/1½ pints boiling water	3¼ cups boiling water
bunch spring onions, chopped	bunch scallions, chopped
a scant teacup chopped fresh parsley	a scant teacup chopped fresh parsley
45 ml/3 tbsps chopped fresh mint	3-4 tbsps chopped fresh mint
75 ml/5 tbsps olive oil	6-7 tbsps olive oil
75 ml/5 tbsps lemon juice	6-7 tbsps lemon juice
freshly ground black pepper	freshly ground black pepper
lettuce	lettuce
tomatoes	tomatoes

Place the bulgar in a saucepan and dry roast over a high heat until it becomes golden brown. Shake the pan frequently to ensure even roasting. Turn out immediately into a heat resistant bowl and add the boiling water. Cover and leave for one hour. The bulgar will become light and fluffy but still have a little resistance to the bite. Drain well and spread onto a clean tea towel, folded in half. Fold in half again, sandwiching the bulgar in the middle. Press firmly to remove any excess moisture. Repeat with another dry cloth if necessary.

Put the 'cooked' bulgar in a large bowl and add

the spring onions, parsley and mint. Mix the olive oil and lemon juice together and pour over. Season with black pepper and toss lightly.

Arrange a few lettuce leaves on a serving dish and spoon on the tabouli. Cut the tomato into thin wedges and use to decorate the dish.

Savouries

Mushroom and Sour Cream Quiche

Metric/Imperial	American
Pastry:	Pastry:
200 g/7 oz wholewheat flour	a scant 1½ cups wholewheat flour
25 g/1 oz soya flour	1½ tbsps soy flour
75 g/3 oz unsalted butter	a scant ½ cup sweet butter
30 ml/2 tbsps sunflower oil	2-3 tbsps sunflower oil
40 ml/8 tsps cold water	8 tsps cold water
Filling:	Filling:
225 g/8 oz button mushrooms	½ lb button mushrooms
½ lemon	½ lemon
freshly ground black pepper	freshly ground black pepper
2 large eggs	2 large eggs
150 ml/5 fl oz sour cream	½ cup sour cream
15 ml/1 tbsp fresh parsley, chopped	1½ tbsps fresh parsley, chopped

To make the pastry, mix the wholewheat and soya flour together in a bowl. Rub in the butter and oil until the mixture resembles breadcrumbs. Add the water and knead to form a dough. Roll out and line an oiled 25 cm/10 inch flan ring.

Press down lightly with the fingertips and prick with a fork. Bake in a preheated oven, gas mark 6 (400°F/200°C) for 10-12 minutes.

Clean and slice the mushrooms and place in a pan with the grated rind and juice of the half lemon. Cover and stew gently for 5-8 minutes. Drain, and reserve the juices. Arrange the mushrooms in the bottom of the blind baked pastry case and season with black pepper. Beat the mushroom juices, eggs and sour cream together and pour over the quiche. Sprinkle with parsley. Bake for 25 minutes.

Tomato Pizza

Metric/Imperial
Base:
225 g/8 oz wholewheat
    flour
15 ml/1 tbsp sunflower oil
15 g/½ oz fresh yeast
150-175 ml/5-6 fl oz warm
    water
additional sunflower oil

Filling:
1 onion
1 green pepper
1 clove garlic, peeled and
    crushed
50 g/2 oz button
    mushrooms, sliced
15 ml/1 tbsp olive oil
450 g/1 lb ripe tomatoes
45 ml/3 tbsps tomato purée
2.5 ml/½ tsp dried basil
2.5 ml/½ tsp dried oregano
freshly ground black
    pepper
Mozzarella cheese, optional

American
Base:
1½ cups wholewheat flour
1½ tbsps sunflower oil
½ tbsp dry active yeast
½-¾ cup warm water
additional sunflower oil

Filling:
1 onion
1 green pepper
1 clove garlic, peeled and
    crushed
½ cup sliced button
    mushrooms
1½ tbsps olive oil
1 lb ripe tomatoes
3-4 tbsps tomato purée
½ tsp dried basil
½ tsp dried oregano
freshly ground black
    pepper
Mozzarella cheese, optional

Put the flour in a mixing bowl and rub in the tablespoon of sunflower oil. Blend the yeast and water together and gradually stir into the flour. Mix to form a dough. Turn out onto a lightly floured board and knead until smooth and elastic. Cover and leave in a warm place to double in size.

Wash, trim and chop the vegetables. Heat the olive oil in a large frying pan and sauté the onion, pepper and garlic until soft. Chop the tomatoes finely or pass through a coarse vegetable mouli. Add to the pan along with the mushrooms, and cook gently for several minutes. Stir in the tomato purée, basil and oregano. Season to taste with black pepper. Bring to the boil. Partially cover with a lid and simmer gently for 15-20 minutes until the mixture thickens. Leave to cool.

When the dough is well risen, knock down and turn out onto a floured board. Roll out to form a rectangle. Brush with oil. Roll up from the shortest side until it resembles a swiss roll. Repeat the rolling, oiling, rolling procedure three times. Keep back a small piece of dough, about the size of a golf ball. Roll out the remainder to form a circle measuring 30 cm/12 inches in diameter. Oil a large baking tray and carefully lift the pizza base onto it. Pinch the edges to make a slightly raised rim and brush with oil.

Spoon the filling mixture over the base. Roll out the remaining dough and cut into strips and lay on top of the pizza to form a lattice. Sprinkle with cheese if desired. Bake in a preheated oven, gas mark 8 (450°F/230°C) for 30-35 minutes.

Spicy Mushroom Pasties

Metric/Imperial	American
100 g/4 oz couscous	1 cup couscous
225 ml/8 fl oz boiling water	1 cup boiling water
30-45 ml/2-3 tbsps sun-flower oil	3-4 tbsps sunflower oil
5 ml/1 tsp black mustard seeds	1 tsp black mustard seeds
5 ml/1 tsp turmeric	1 tsp turmeric
2 fresh green chillies, finely chopped	2 fresh green chilies, finely chopped
225 g/8 oz mushrooms, sliced	2 cups sliced mushrooms
5 ml/1 tsp garam masala	1 tsp garam masala
juice of 1 lemon	juice of 1 lemon
450 g/1 lb wholewheat short crust pastry	1 lb wholewheat short crust pastry

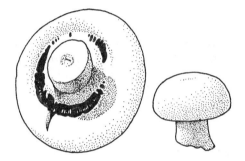

Dry roast the couscous in a pan over a high heat until golden brown. Place immediately in bowl and cover with the boiling water. Leave for 10-15 minutes until all the water has been absorbed and the couscous is light and fluffy.

Heat the oil in a large frying pan and stir in the mustard seeds, turmeric and fresh chilli. Fry gently for 5 minutes. Add the mushrooms and cook for a further 5 minutes. Stir in the garam masala, lemon juice and couscous.

Preheat the oven to gas mark 6 (400°F/200°C).

Roll out the pastry and cut into 8 circles, measuring 15 cm/6 inches in diameter. Put a little of the filling on one side of each round. Fold over the other side. Dampen the edges and press together to seal. Place on a floured baking tray and bake for 25 minutes.

Samosas

Samosas are crisp pastry triangles filled with spiced vegetables. They can be eaten hot or cold as hors d'oeuvres, as a side dish to accompany a curry, as a snack and on picnics. It is worthwhile making more than you need at any one time for they freeze very well.

This recipe, given to me by an Indian friend, uses the spice asafoetida. It has a rather pungent, garlicky smell and it is hard to imagine how such an ingredient can be used to advantage in the kitchen. Apparently asafoetida enhances the flavour of more aromatic spices and without it many Indian dishes would simply not be authentic. I am also told that it aids the digestion and is used medicinally for upset stomachs.

makes 15

Metric/Imperial
Filling:
150 ml/5 fl oz sunflower oil
5 ml/1 tsp black mustard seeds
2.5 ml/½ tsp asafoetida
2 carrots, sliced
2 potatoes, diced
225 g/8 oz peas
2 green chillies, finely chopped
5 ml/1 tsp lemon juice
5 ml/1 tsp turmeric
15 ml/1 tbsp fresh coriander, chopped
freshly ground black pepper

American
Filling:
½ cup sunflower oil
1 tsp black mustard seeds
½ tsp asafoetida
2 carrots, sliced
2 potatoes, diced
½ lb peas
2 green chillies, finely chopped
1 tsp lemon juice
1 tsp turmeric
1½ tbsps fresh coriander, chopped
freshly ground black pepper

Pastry:
150 g/5 oz fine wholewheat flour
100 g/4 oz unbleached white flour
15 ml/1 tbsp sunflower oil
150 ml/5 fl oz warm water
additional flour
additional oil
oil for deep frying

Pastry:
1 cup fine wholewheat flour
¾ cup unbleached white all-purpose flour
1½ tbsps sunflower oil
½ cup warm water
additional flour
additional oil
oil for deep frying

To make the filling heat the oil in a large pan and fry the mustard seeds for 2-3 minutes. Stir in the asafoetida and fry for a further minute or two. Add the vegetables and cook gently for 10-15 minutes until they begin to soften. Toss in the chillies and fry for 5 minutes more. Add the remaining filling ingredients and season with black pepper. Leave aside until needed.

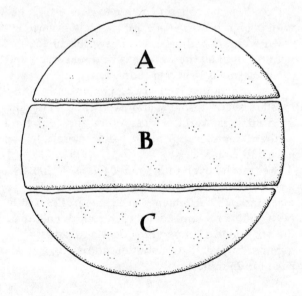

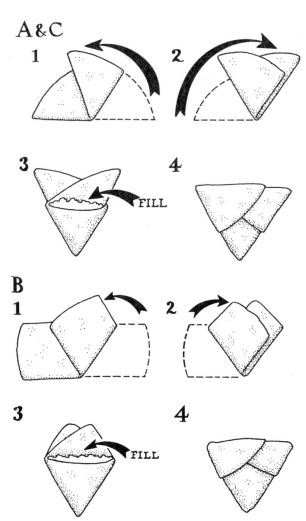

A&C

1

2

3   FILL

4

B

1

2

3   FILL

4

Mix the wholewheat and unbleached white flours together in a bowl. Rub in the oil and gradually add the water to form a soft dough. Break into 5 pieces and roll into small balls. Roll out as if making chapati. Cover with a damp cloth. Lightly dust a pastry board or work surface and place a 'chapati' in the centre. Brush with oil and lightly dust with flour. Place another 'chapati' on top, oil and dust with flour. Lay a third 'chapati' on top. Roll out to twice their original size. Cover with a damp cloth. Repeat the process with the remaining 'chapati', making a stack of 2 rather than 3 'chapati'. Roll out.

Heat a tarva or large cast iron frying pan. Carefully separate the 'chapati', peeling them one from another. You should now have 5 large but very thin 'chapati'. Cook each one lightly, until they lose their translucent appearance. Cut and fold as illustrated.

Mix together a little flour and water to make a stiff paste or glue. Place 15 ml/1 tbsp of filling into each cone. Fold over the top flap and seal the seams with a little paste. The package should resemble a neat, stuffed triangle. Deep fry until golden brown. Drain on absorbent paper.

Rice Balls

In Britain and America most of the millet is found in pet shops where it is sold as bird food. I remember, when working in a wholefood shop some years ago, the look of horror on one customer's face when he learned that I ate millet — he bought it for his racing pigeons!

It is a great pity that millet is held in such low regard for it is a pleasant, highly nutritious grain and one that is still the staple food in many parts of Africa, Asia and India. I like its nutty flavour and light, fluffy texture and use it regularly in a wide variety of dishes.

When cooked it resembles couscous although it is yellower in colour. To bring out the full flavour of millet and to reduce the cooking time I dry roast the grain before simmering in water. Simply put the grain in an old pan over a hot flame. Shake the pan frequently to ensure even roasting and continue to cook until the millet becomes a little darker in colour. Tip from the pan as soon as it is ready to prevent it from burning. Simmer in twice its volume of water for 15 minutes until light and fluffy.

Metric/Imperial	American
175 g/6 oz short grain brown rice, cooked	1 cup short grain brown rice, cooked
100 g/4 oz millet, cooked	1 cup millet, cooked
3 carrots, grated	3 carrots, grated
100 g/4 oz mushrooms, finely chopped	1 cup mushrooms, finely chopped
1 bunch spring onions, chopped	1 bunch scallions, chopped
30 ml/2 tbsps fresh sage, chopped	2-3 tbsps fresh sage, chopped
30 ml/2 tbsps fresh savory, chopped	2-3 tbsps fresh savory, chopped
freshly ground black pepper	freshly ground black pepper

Preheat the oven to gas mark 5 (375°F/190°C).

Mix all the ingredients together in a large bowl. Squeeze between the fingers until the mixture is sticky. Press together to form balls, slightly smaller than tennis balls. Place on an oiled baking tray and cook for 25-30 minutes until golden brown.

Serve hot or cold. They also freeze well.

Hazel Nut Rissoles

Makes 6-8

Metric/Imperial
1 onion, finely chopped
2 carrots, finely grated
1 green pepper, finely
  chopped
75 g/3 oz roasted hazel
  nuts, coarsely ground
60-75 ml/4-5 tbsps soft
  wholewheat breadcrumbs
5 ml/1 tsp dried mixed
  herbs
15 ml/1 tbsp natural
  yoghurt
15 ml/1 tbsp tomato purée
1 large egg, beaten
freshly ground black
  pepper

To coat:
soft wholewheat bread-
  crumbs
1 egg, beaten

American
1 onion, finely chopped
2 carrots, finely grated
1 green pepper, finely
  chopped
¾ cup roasted hazel nuts,
  coarsely ground
5-7 tbsps soft wholewheat
  breadcrumbs
1 tsp dried mixed herbs
1½ tbsps unflavored yogurt
1½ tbsps tomato purée
1 large egg, beaten
freshly ground black
  pepper

To coat:
soft wholewheat bread-
  crumbs
1 egg, beaten

Preheat the oven to gas mark 4 (350°F/180°C).
Mix all the ingredients together in a bowl.
Season to taste. Shape into rissoles. Brush with the
remaining beaten egg and roll in the breadcrumbs.
Place on a greased baking tray and bake for 15
minutes on each side until golden brown. They
can also be fried in a little oil.
   Serve with a sauce of your choice e.g. tomato,
bechamel, mushroom.

Brazil Nut Burgers

Makes 8

Metric/Imperial
15-30 ml/1-2 tbsps groundnut oil
1 onion, sliced
2.5 cm/1 inch fresh root
  ginger, peeled and grated
175 g /6 oz mushrooms,
  finely chopped
100 g/4 oz brazil nuts,
  coarsely ground
1 carrot, grated
100 g/4 oz soft wholewheat
  breadcrumbs
30 ml/2 tbsps tahini
15 ml/1 tbsp fresh
  rosemary, chopped
oil for frying

American
1½-3 tbsps peanut oil
1 onion, sliced
1 inch fresh ginger root,
  peeled and grated
1½ cups finely chopped
  mushrooms
1 cup brazil nuts, coarsely
  ground
1 carrot, grated
1 cup soft wholewheat
  breadcrumbs
2-3 tbsps tahini
1½ tbsps fresh rosemary,
  chopped
oil for frying

   Heat the groundnut oil in a pan and lightly fry
the onion and ginger until soft. Add the
mushrooms and cook for a further 3-4 minutes.
Remove from the heat and stir in the remaining
ingredients. Shape into flat burgers and fry until
golden brown on both sides.
   Serve with sautéed potatoes, vegetables and a
sauce.

Hazel Nut Pâté

Metric/Imperial
225 g/8 oz ground hazel nuts
2 eating apples, grated
50 g/2 oz natural cottage cheese
50 g/2 oz soft wholewheat breadcrumbs
10 ml/2 tsps lemon juice
30 ml/2 tbsps fresh chives, finely chopped
freshly ground black pepper

American
2 cups ground hazel nuts
2 eating apples, grated
¼ cup unflavored cottage cheese
½ cup soft wholewheat breadcrumbs
2 tsps lemon juice
2-3 tbsps fresh chives, finely chopped
freshly ground black pepper

Pass the hazel nuts, grated apple, cottage cheese and breadcrumbs through a fine vegetable mouli. Stir in the lemon juice and chives and season to taste with black pepper. Press into a small pot.
Serve with wholewheat toast and a green salad.

Home-Made Peanut Butter

Put a cupful of roasted peanuts into a liquidiser. Add 5-10 ml/1-2 tsps of peanut oil and blend until crunchy or smooth, according to taste.

Breadmaking

I bake all my own bread and, for me, breadmaking is one of the most enjoyable and satisfying tasks. Having produced my fair share of 'building bricks' the appearance and smell of three well-risen, freshly baked loaves never fail to give me a feeling of pleasure and satisfaction.

Although I enjoy donning my 'master baker's hat' there are times when it is inconvenient, and it would be nice to be able to pop round the corner to the supermarket or bakers for a loaf. Unfortunately there are very few shops that sell unsalted bread let alone good wholewheat bread without other additives.

I use a finely-ground organically grown stoneground 100% wholewheat flour. Although coarsely milled flour may look more wholesome it is much more difficult to handle and can result in heavy loaves. One common difficulty experienced by breadmakers using wholewheat flour is crumbly bread which is difficult to slice. I haven't experienced this problem and can only hazard a guess as to its cause. It may be a result of proving the dough too quickly, proving for too long, using too much fat or using flour that is too fresh. Many professional bakers, buying direct from local millers, leave the flour to mature for several weeks before using it.

Other common problems are:

1. Bread failing to rise — yeast can be killed by using too hot water or proving in too hot a place. Very cold conditions will inactivate the yeast.
2. Crust coming away from the loaf — the dough may not have been kneaded sufficiently or may have been proved too quickly.
3. Dry, heavy bread — too dry a mixture or overcooking.
4. Bread uncooked in the middle — too wet a dough or insufficient cooking.
5. Bread that rises and then collapses — over-proving.
6. Bread that has a flat, pitted crust — too wet a dough.

I use neither sugar nor salt when making bread. Omitting the sugar makes no difference to the taste, texture or quality of the bread. Omitting the salt from one's bread however is a more controversial subject. Some people believe it to be an essential ingredient, as vital to the mixture as the yeast itself.

It is interesting to hear criticisms of 'unpalatable', 'horrible' and 'bland' being voiced about unsalted bread for there can be few people who have ever actually tasted salt-free bread. Salt is added, without question, to most commercial and home-made breads. I certainly hadn't tasted salt-free bread until I decided to leave the salt out of my usual bread mix. The result was a revelation — a delicious, well-risen loaf. It tasted slightly sweeter than normal but my long-suffering husband ate it without comment. After all, as far as he was concerned, it was just another loaf which merited neither praise nor criticism. My bread has been salt-free ever since, and commercially produced bread now tastes excessively salty to our palates.

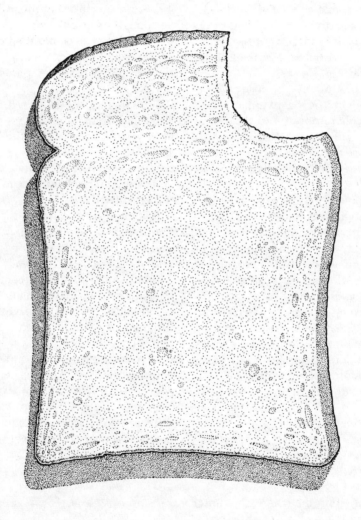

Wholewheat Bread

Makes 3 loaves

Metric/Imperial	American
50 g/2 oz fresh yeast	2-3 tbsps dry active yeast
850 ml/1½ pints warm water	3¼ cups warm water
1½ kg/3 lbs wholewheat flour	10 cups wholewheat flour
15 ml/1 tbsp sunflower oil	1½ tbsps sunflower oil

Cream the yeast with 275 ml/½ pint (1 cup) warm water and 100 g/4 oz (1 cup) flour. Leave for 10 minutes in a warm place until the mixture begins to froth.

Mix the remaining flour and oil together in a large bowl and stir in the rest of the warm water and the yeast mixture. Mix to form a dough and knead until smooth and elastic. Return to the bowl and cover with a polythene bag. Leave in a warm place to double in size.

Turn onto a lightly floured board and knead again. Cut into three and roll into shape. Place in three oiled (900 g/2 lb) bread tins, cover and leave in a warm place to double in size. Bake in a preheated oven, gas mark 6 (400°F/200°C) for 40 minutes.

Because many wholewheat flours are low in gluten it is not really necessary to prove the bread twice. In fact I now miss out the first rise and simply put the freshly kneaded dough straight into oiled tins, leave it to rise and then bake it as usual.

Granary Rolls

Metric/Imperial	American
15 g/½ oz fresh yeast	½ tbsp dry active yeast
450 g/1 lb granary flour	3 cups granary flour
275 ml/10 fl oz tepid milk and water, mixed	1¼ cups tepid milk and water, mixed
15 ml/1 tbsp sunflower oil	1½ tbsps sunflower oil
flour for dredging	flour for dredging

Cream the yeast with 100 g/4 oz (1 cup) flour and 150 ml/5 fl oz (½ cup) of tepid liquid. Leave in a warm place to froth.

Add the remaining ingredients and mix to form a dough. Knead on a floured board until smooth and elastic. Put the dough in an oiled bowl and cover with a polythene bag. Leave in a warm place to double in size.

Turn the dough onto a floured board and knead lightly for 1-2 minutes. Cut into eight pieces and roll into shape. Place on a floured baking tray and flatten slightly with the fingertips. Cover and leave to prove until well risen.

Dredge the rolls lightly with flour and bake in a preheated oven, gas mark 6 (400°F/200°C) for 15-20 minutes.

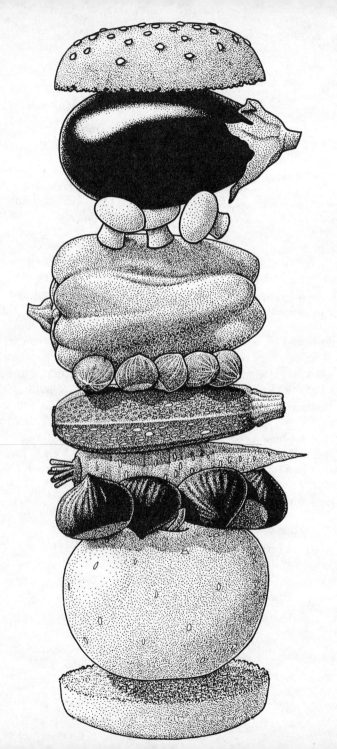

Vegetarian Dishes

Chestnut Stroganoff

Metric/Imperial	American
8 large prunes	8 large prunes
275 ml/10 fl oz red wine	1¼ cups red wine
675 g/1½ lbs chestnuts	1½ lbs chestnuts
60 ml/4 tbsps olive oil	5-6 tbsps olive oil
3 onions, sliced	3 onions, sliced
675 g/1½ lbs red cabbage, shredded	1½ lbs red cabbage, shredded
2 cooking apples, cored and sliced	2 cooking apples, cored and sliced
30 ml/2 tbsps lemon juice	2-3 tbsps lemon juice
a pinch cayenne pepper	a pinch cayenne pepper
a pinch chilli pepper	a pinch chili pepper
a pinch paprika	a pinch paprika
freshly ground black pepper	freshly ground black pepper

Soak the prunes overnight in the wine. Drain and reserve the juice. Stone and chop the prunes. Prepare the chestnuts as described on page 33.

Preheat the oven to gas mark 6 (400°F/200°C).

Heat the oil in a large pan and sauté the onions until soft and golden coloured. Add the remaining ingredients including the prunes, juice/wine and cooked and peeled chestnuts. Transfer to an ovenproof casserole and cover. Bake for 45-50 minutes. Adjust the seasoning to taste.

Serve with baked potatoes and sour cream.

Chestnut and Mushroom en Croûte

Metric/Imperial
Filling:
450 g/1 lb chestnuts
2 onions
1 clove garlic, peeled and
    crushed
225 g/8 oz button
    mushrooms, chopped
4 large tomatoes
30 ml/2 tbsps olive oil
1.25 ml/¼ tsp freshly
    grated nutmeg

sauce:
575 ml/1 pint milk
10 black peppercorns
2 slices of onion
½ carrot, sliced
1 bay leaf
30 g/1¼ oz unsalted butter
25 g/1 oz wholewheat flour
10 ml/ 2 tsps Dijon
    mustard

Pastry:
275 g/10 oz wholewheat
    flour
75 g/3 oz unsalted butter
30 ml/2 tbsps sunflower oil
30 ml/2 tbsps corn oil
50 ml/10 tsps cold water

to glaze:
1 egg, beaten

American
Filling:
1 lb chestnuts
2 onions
1 clove garlic, peeled and
    crushed
2 cups button mushrooms,
    chopped
4 large tomatoes
2-3 tbsps olive oil
¼ tsp freshly grated
    nutmeg

sauce:
2½ cups milk
10 black peppercorns
2 slices of onion
½ carrot, sliced
1 bay leaf
3 tbsps sweet butter
1½ tbsps wholewheat flour
2 tsps Dijon mustard

Pastry:
2 cups wholewheat flour
a scant ½ cup sweet butter
2-3 tbsps sunflower oil
2-3 tbsps corn oil
10 tsps cold water

to glaze:
1 egg, beaten

Prepare the chestnuts as directed on page 33.

Wash and slice the vegetables and sauté the onion and garlic in the olive oil until soft. Add the mushrooms and tomatoes and cook for a further 4-5 minutes. Stir in the peeled chestnuts and the ground nutmeg. Place in a large pie dish.

To make the sauce put the milk, peppercorns, onion, carrot and bay leaf in a pan and bring to the boil. Remove from the heat and leave aside for 15 minutes. Then strain and reserve the milk. Wipe the pan clean and melt the butter. Stir in the flour and cook for 1-2 minutes. Remove from the heat and gradually stir in the milk. Bring to the boil slowly, stirring all the time. Mix in the mustard. Pour the sauce over the vegetable and chestnut mixture.

To make the pastry put the flour in a bowl and rub in the butter and oil until the mixture resembles breadcrumbs. Add the cold water and mix together to form a pastry dough. Roll out on a lightly floured board and place on top of the pie filling. Dampen the pastry edges and press to seal. Brush with beaten egg and bake in a preheated oven, gas mark 6 (400°F/200°C) for 25-30 minutes.

Serve with baked potatoes and lightly cooked carrots and breaded sprouts.

Brown Rice

There are many schools of thought regarding the best way to prepare rice. Some people wash it, soak it and even dry roast it before cooking. Some cook it with salt, some boil it in an open saucepan while others believe that a final rinsing in water gives the best results. I am sure that you too have your own tried and tested method which I have no wish to contradict but I will give some basic guidelines for preparing brown rice which cooks slightly differently to white varieties.

While many people appreciate the nutty flavour, slightly chewy texture, visual appeal and dietary value of natural brown rice the transition from white to brown is not always smooth. The two principal areas of complaint are usually that cooked brown rice either becomes too soft and stodgy or remains as hard as little bullets.

I have carried out an experiment in which I cooked two quantities of rice in the same amount of water, first in a heavy, enamelled cast iron pan with a tight-fitting lid and then in a lighter aluminium pan. The difference was most impressive. The rice simmered in the heavy pan cooked to perfection. It was tender, dry, separate and held its shape. On the other hand the rice cooked in the lighter pan took longer to cook, needed more water and did not cook evenly — becoming soft and soggy at the bottom of the pan and hard and chewy at the top.

As well as using a good heavy pan I suggest that you also measure the rice into a mug or cup and cook it in twice as much water. A useful guide is that one mugful of uncooked rice weighs approximately 225 g/½ lb and will yield 675 g/1½ lbs when cooked. I find this quantity sufficient for 3-4 people.

Plain Boiled Rice

1 cup long grain brown rice
2 cups water

Wash the rice thoroughly in cold water. Drain and place in a heavy pan. Add the water and bring to the boil. Cover and simmer gently for 35-40 minutes (short grain brown rice takes 5-10 minutes more). Do not stir once it has begun to cook as this breaks the soft bran layer causing the rice to become sticky. At the end of the cooking period push a blunt-ended utensil into the rice to check whether all the water has been absorbed. Test a grain or two. The rice should be dry and tender but with a little resistance to the bite. Replace the lid as quickly as possible and remove from the heat. Leave to stand for 10 minutes. Stir with a wooden fork or rice paddle before serving.

Pilau Rice

Metric/Imperial	*American*
50 g/2 oz unsalted butter/ ghee	¼ cup sweet butter/ghee
6 whole cloves	6 whole cloves
5 cm/2 inches cinnamon stick	2 inches cinnamon stick
2.5 ml/½ tsp turmeric	½ tsp turmeric
2.5 ml/½ tsp ground coriander	½ tsp ground coriander
2.5 ml/½ tsp cumin seeds	½ tsp cumin seeds
2.5 cm/1 inch fresh root ginger, peeled and grated	1 inch fresh ginger root, peeled and grated
1 bay leaf	1 bay leaf
50 g/2 oz raisins	½ cup raisins
50 g/2 oz pine kernels	½ cup pine kernels (pignoli)
175 g/6 oz long grain brown rice	1 cup long grain brown rice
425 ml/15 fl oz water	1¾ cups water

Melt the butter in a large, heavy pan. Stir in the spices and root ginger and fry lightly for 2-3 minutes. Add the bay leaf, raisins, pine kernels and rice and cook for a further 5 minutes, stirring frequently to coat the rice evenly with butter. Pour in the water, cover the pan and bring to the boil. Simmer for 35-40 minutes until the rice is cooked. Remove from the heat, replace the lid and leave to stand for 5-10 minutes.

The cloves, cinnamon stick and bay leaf are removed during the course of the meal by those unlucky enough to find them on their plates!

Serve with a meat or vegetable curry.

Brown Rice with Leeks and Herbs

Metric/Imperial	*American*
2 leeks	2 leeks
15 g/½ oz unsalted butter	1½ tbsps sweet butter
30 ml/2 tbsps sunflower oil	2-3 tbsps sunflower oil
175 g/6 oz long grain brown rice	1 cup long grain brown rice
425 ml/15 fl oz water	1¾ cups water
juice of ½ lemon	juice of ½ lemon
10 ml/2 tsps Dijon mustard	2 tsps Dijon mustard
15 ml/1 tbsp fresh parsley, chopped	1½ tbsps fresh parsley, chopped
15 ml/1 tbsp fresh chives, chopped	1½ tbsps fresh chives, chopped
freshly ground black pepper	freshly ground black pepper

Wash, trim and slice the leeks. Heat the butter and oil in a heavy pan and sauté the leeks lightly for 5-8 minutes. Add the rice and toss well to coat it evenly in the oil. Pour over the water and lemon juice and stir in the mustard. Cover and bring to the boil. Simmer for 35-40 minutes. Stir in the herbs and replace the lid. Leave for 5-10 minutes. Season to taste with freshly ground black pepper.

Vegetable Kitchiri

In spite of the bewildering array of lentils on sale in some shops I am sure most people are able to recognise the three main types; the whole brown lentil, the whole green lentil and the split red lentil. However in this recipe I use another variety, sold locally as Continental or Puy lentil. It is a small, round, dark green/black pulse and is easy to identify because it is smaller than the average brown lentil and much darker than the green lentil.

Sort through the lentils and split peas and remove any small stones. Put in a pan with plenty of water and bring to the boil. Simmer for 12 minutes. Drain and put aside.

Heat the oil in a large pan and fry the onion until golden brown. Add the garlic and the chilli and cook for a further 2-3 minutes. Stir in the spices and fry for a few moments more. Add the vegetables and sauté for 5 minutes, stirring frequently. Add the parboiled lentils, the brown rice, water and grated coconut. Cover and bring to the boil. Simmer for 35-40 minutes until the rice and lentils are tender and all the water has been absorbed. Sprinkle with fresh coriander.

Serve with chapati.

Metric/Imperial
75 g/3 oz Puy lentils
50 g/2 oz red lentils
50 g/2 oz yellow split peas
75 ml/5 tbsps sunflower oil/ghee
1 onion, chopped
2 cloves garlic, peeled and crushed
2 green chillies, finely chopped
15 ml/1 tbsp ground coriander
5 ml/1 tsp black mustard seeds
2.5 ml/½ tsp turmeric
1 potato, diced
1 carrot, diced
1 small aubergine, diced
¼ head cauliflower, chopped
2 tomatoes, chopped
100 g/4 oz green peas
225 g/8 oz long grain brown rice
575 ml/1 pint water
25 g/1 oz creamed coconut, grated
15 ml/1 tbsp fresh coriander, chopped

American
a scant ½ cup Puy lentils
¼ cup red lentils
¼ cup yellow split peas
6-7 tbsps vegetable oil/ghee
1 onion, chopped
2 cloves garlic, peeled and crushed
2 green chilies, finely chopped
1½ tbsps ground coriander
1 tsp black mustard seeds
½ tsp turmeric
1 potato, diced
1 carrot, diced
1 small egg plant, diced
¼ head cauliflower, chopped
2 tomatoes, chopped
½ cup green peas
1⅓ cups long grain brown rice
2½ cups water
2-3 tbsps grated creamed coconut
1½ tbsps fresh coriander, chopped

Chapter

Chapati

This unleavened bread is traditionally served with Indian curries and savoury dishes. Chapati are made from very finely ground wholewheat flour sold as chapati flour or ata in Indian shops. They are cooked on a tarva, a slightly concave circular cast iron griddle that is pre-heated before the chapati is placed on it. This preheating helps to keep the chapati soft and pliant. If you can't get such a pan (Indian hardware shops sell them very cheaply) use a cast iron frying pan.

Cooking the chapati is easy in comparison to the task of rolling out a succession of thin, evenly shaped discs of dough. The secret lies in the use of a specially shaped rolling pin, that looks a little like a chair rung, being thicker in the centre than at the ends and much thinner than conventional western rolling pins. By applying a little pressure to one side of the rolling pin the chapati dough rotates round the floured board, becoming thinner and larger as the rolling continues. Many Indian women spend up to an hour every day making chapati for their families. It is a joy to watch them at work and to see the pile of identical chapati steadily rising beneath the cloth which covers them to keep them clean and moist.

Makes 10-12 chapati

Metric/Imperial	American
250 g/9 oz chapati flour	1¾ cups chapati flour
15 ml/1 tbsp sunflower oil	1½ tbsps sunflower oil
150 ml/5 fl oz warm water (approx)	½ cup warm water (approx)

Place the flour in a bowl and rub in the oil. Gradually add the water to form a soft dough. Chapati dough has to be quite soft, the amount of water required varying with the type of flour. Knead for a few minutes until smooth and elastic.

Place the tarva or frying pan on a medium heat for 10 minutes. Divide the dough into 10-12 small balls and roll out each one on a well-floured board until it measures about 15 cm/6 inches in diameter. Shake off any surplus flour before cooking.

Cook on one side until speckled brown, turn over and cook for half a minute on the second side. Take the pan off the stove and throw the chapati directly on top of a low flame. It should puff up. Remove and keep under a clean cloth until needed.

To make a richer chapati rub both sides with a little butter after cooking but before stacking under the cloth.

Spiced Blackeye Beans with Mushrooms

This is one of my favourite curried dishes, with a delicious flavour and also easy to prepare. Blackeye beans are slightly bigger than haricots but require no preliminary soaking and will cook in about 45 minutes. Obviously if you have a pressure cooker the time is greatly reduced — about 10 minutes at high pressure.

Metric/Imperial	American
175 g/6 oz blackeye beans	¾ cup blackeye beans
30 ml/2 tbsps groundnut oil	2-3 tbsps peanut oil
2 onions, sliced	2 onions, sliced
2 cloves garlic, peeled and crushed	2 cloves garlic, peeled and crushed
5 cm/2 inches fresh root ginger, peeled and grated	2 inches fresh ginger root, peeled and grated
10 ml/2 tsps black mustard seeds	2 tsps black mustard seeds
5 ml/1 tsp cumin seeds	1 tsp cumin seeds
4 tomatoes, chopped	4 tomatoes, chopped
225 g/8 oz mushrooms, chopped	½ lb mushrooms, chopped
5 ml/1 tsp ground coriander	1 tsp ground coriander
10 ml/2 tsps turmeric	2 tsps turmeric
15 ml/1 tbsp fresh coriander, chopped	1½ tbsps fresh coriander, chopped

Place the beans in a pan or pressure cooker with plenty of water and cook until tender. Heat the oil in a large frying pan. Add the onions, garlic and root ginger and sauté gently for 10 minutes, stirring frequently. Stir in the mustard seeds and cumin seeds and fry for a further 5 minutes. Add the tomatoes, mushrooms, ground coriander and turmeric and cook gently until the juices begin to run. Add the cooked beans and a spoonful or two of bean stock. The curry should be moist rather than wet. Sprinkle with fresh coriander.

Serve with brown rice or chapati.

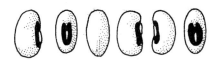

Crusty Lentil and Vegetable Ring

Metric/Imperial
Filling:
1 onion
4 whole cloves
1 bay leaf
100 g/4 oz green lentils
275 ml/10 fl oz water
15 ml/1 tbsp olive oil
225 g/8 oz leeks, thinly
    sliced
50 g/2 oz mushrooms,
    sliced
5 ml/1 tsp fresh mint,
    chopped
5 ml/1 tsp fresh parsley,
    chopped
10 ml/2 tsps lemon juice
freshly ground black
    pepper

Pastry:
225 g/ 8 oz wholewheat
    flour
100 g/4 oz firm unsalted
    butter
75-90 ml/5-6 tbsps cold
    water

to glaze:
1 egg, beaten

American
filling:
1 onion
4 whole cloves
1 bay leaf
½ cup green lentils
1¼ cups water
1½ tbsps olive oil
½ lb leeks, thinly sliced
½ cup sliced mushrooms
1 tsp fresh mint, chopped
1 tsp fresh parsley,
    chopped
2 tsps lemon juice
freshly ground black
    pepper

Pastry:
1½ cups wholewheat flour
½ cup firm sweet butter
6-9 tbsps cold water

To glaze:
1 egg, beaten

Push the cloves into the peeled onion and place in a pan with the bay leaf, green lentils and water. Simmer for 45-50 minutes or pressure cook for 10-12 minutes until tender. Drain. Remove the cloves and the bay leaf and chop the onion.

Heat the oil in a pan and sauté the leeks and mushrooms until soft. Add the chopped onion, cooked lentils, mint, parsley, lemon juice and a little black pepper. Adjust seasoning to taste. Leave to cool. Drain well and reserve any stock to make into a gravy to serve with the dish.

To make the pastry place the flour in a bowl. Grate in the butter and add sufficient water to make a stiff dough. Roll out on a lightly floured board to form an oblong 20 cm × 40 cm (8 ins × 16 ins). Place the pastry on a greased baking tray and spoon over the filling mixture, leaving a 2.5 cm (1 inch) gap round the edge. Moisten the pastry edge with a little water and roll up like a swiss roll. Twist to form a ring or circle. Make a series of cuts in the pastry top, 5 cm (2 inches) apart.

Brush with beaten egg and bake in a preheated oven, gas mark 6 (400°F/200°C) for 30 minutes.

Serve with potatoes en papillotes and lightly cooked carrots.

Chick Pea Blanquette

Metric/Imperial	*American*
175 g/6 oz chick peas, soaked overnight	¾ cup chick peas, soaked overnight
850 ml/1½ pints water	3¼ cups water
30 ml/2 tbsps sunflower oil	2-3 tbsps sunflower oil
2 onions, chopped	2 onions, chopped
2 leeks, chopped	2 leeks, chopped
1 clove garlic, peeled and crushed	1 clove garlic, peeled and crushed
225g/8 oz mushrooms, sliced	½ lb mushrooms, sliced
juice of 1 lemon	juice of 1 lemon
30 ml/2 tbsps tahini	2-3 tbsps tahini
275-350 ml/10-12 fl oz bean stock	1¼-1½ cups bean stock
15-30 ml/1-2 tbsps fresh mint, chopped	1½-3 tbsps fresh mint, chopped
15-30 ml/1-2 tbsps fresh thyme, chopped	1½-3 tbsps fresh thyme, chopped
freshly ground black pepper	freshly ground black pepper

Drain the chick peas and simmer in the water for 1½-2 hours until tender. They will cook in 20-25 minutes in a pressure cooker at high pressure. Drain and reserve the bean stock. Rub half the cooked beans through a sieve or vegetable mouli and discard the skins.

Heat the oil in a pan and soften the onion, leeks and garlic for 5-10 minutes. Add the mushrooms and cook until their juices begin to run. Blend the lemon juice, tahini, bean stock and puréed beans together before pouring over the sautéed vegetables. Add the remaining chick peas, the thyme and mint, and a little black pepper. Adjust the seasoning to taste. Heat through.

Serve with rice balls or pasta.

Couscous

To avoid confusion it must be explained that couscous is the name given to a product made from semolina and also to a delicious stew, popular in North Africa. I first ate couscous at a market café in the old quarter of Marrakesh surrounded by Bedouin arabs and dark skinned Africans. Everyone there seemed to be eating the rich, spiced stew made from vegetables, chick peas and mutton, served with a veritable mountain of light fluffy grain.

The grain which accompanied the stew is also called couscous in Europe and North America where it can be bought, ready-to-cook, in many food stores. It is becoming increasingly popular because of the ease and speed with which it can be cooked. Simply place 1 part couscous in a bowl and pour over 2 parts boiling water. Leave to stand for 10-15 minutes during which time it will absorb all the water, soften and double in volume. The bowl can be placed in a hot oven to keep the couscous warm or the soaked grain can be steamed, uncovered, until heated through.

For those of you with plenty of time and an adventurous nature conscous can be made at home. You will need equal amounts of fine and coarse semolina. As for the method I place you in the capable hands of Tom Stobart who gave the following instructions in his book, *The Cook's Encyclopaedia*.

'Have ready a basin of water, a shallow dish of semolina (a mixture of coarse and fine) and a clean cloth spread on the table. Touch the palm of the right hand into the water to wet it slightly. Then lay it on the semolina mixture so that some of it sticks to the palm and rub one palm against the other, finishing with a circular movement to roughly round the grains. Then let the grains fall on the cloth. Naturally the touch must be light or the grains will become dough. The fine particles of semolina are of course necessary to make the coarse ones stick together. The final operation is to sieve out any surplus flour or fine bits and to let the couscous dry.'

To cook home-made couscous moisten with water and allow the grains to swell. Spoon into a couscousier or a steamer lined with muslin. Place over the 'stew' at least one hour before the completed cooking time. Do not cover the steamer otherwise condensation will drop onto the couscous making it soggy and lumpy. The stew and the couscous should be ready to serve at the same time.

Vegetarian Couscous

Metric/Imperial	American
30 ml/2 tbsps groundnut oil	2-3 tbsps peanut oil
1 clove garlic, peeled and crushed	1 clove garlic, peeled and crushed
2.5 cm/1 inch fresh root ginger, peeled and grated	1 inch fresh ginger root, peeled and grated
1 onion, sliced	1 onion, sliced
1 green chilli, finely chopped	1 green chili, finely chopped
10 ml/2 tsps ground cumin	2 tsps ground cumin
10 ml/2 tsps turmeric	2 tsps turmeric
10 ml/2 tsps ground coriander	2 tsps ground coriander
5 ml/1 tsp paprika	1 tsp paprika
2 courgettes, sliced	2 zucchini, sliced
1 red pepper, sliced	1 red pepper, sliced
1 aubergine, chopped	1 egg plant, chopped
1 potato, chopped	1 potato, chopped
4 carrots, sliced	4 carrots, sliced
3 tomatoes, sliced	3 tomatoes, sliced
225 g/8 oz chick peas, cooked	1 cup chick peas, cooked
50 g/2 oz raisins	½ cup raisins
50 g/2 oz blanched almonds, chopped	½ cup blanched almonds, chopped
350 g/12 oz couscous	3 cups couscous

Heat the oil in a large, heavy pan and gently fry the garlic, ginger and onion until soft. Stir in the green chilli and spices and continue frying for another 5 minutes, stirring frequently. Add the vegetables and just cover with water. Bring to the boil and simmer until soft. Add the remaining ingredients EXCEPT for the couscous and cook for a further 15 minutes.

Meanwhile soak the couscous as described on the previous page and heat through ready to serve. Pile the hot couscous around a large serving dish and spoon the stew into the centre.
Serve.

Couscous Topped with Vegetables and Yoghurt

Metric/Imperial
175 g/6 oz couscous, soaked
30 ml/2 tbsps olive oil
1 clove garlic, peeled and crushed
1 onion, sliced
225 g/8 oz leeks, sliced
1 parsnip, thinly sliced
2 carrots, thinly sliced
225 g/8 oz tomatoes, sliced
150 ml/5 fl oz water
15 ml/1 tbsp fresh thyme, chopped
freshly ground black pepper
1 egg
275 ml/10 fl oz natural yoghurt
15 ml/1 tbsp unbleached white flour

American
1½ cups couscous, soaked
2-3 tbsps olive oil
1 clove garlic, peeled and crushed
1 onion, sliced
½ lb leeks, sliced
1 parsnip, thinly sliced
2 carrots, thinly sliced
½ lb tomatoes, sliced
½ cup water
1½ tbsps fresh thyme, chopped
freshly ground black pepper
1 egg
1¼ cups unflavored yogurt
1½ tbsps unbleached all-purpose white flour

Place the soaked couscous in the bottom of a lightly oiled casserole dish. Heat the oil in a pan and gently sauté the garlic and onion until soft. Add the other vegetables and toss lightly to coat in oil. Pour in the water and cook until tender. The mixture should be relatively dry so boil vigorously to reduce the stock if necessary. Season with fresh thyme and black pepper. Spoon over the couscous.

Beat the egg, yoghurt and flour together and pour over the vegetables. Bake in a preheated oven, gas mark 4 (350°F/180°C) for 30 minutes until firm to touch.

Serve with a side salad and granary rolls.

Mediterranean Ragoût with Vegetables

Metric/Imperial
1 large onion
1 clove garlic, peeled and crushed
2 carrots
225 g/8 oz leeks
2 courgettes
¼ head cauliflower
225 g/8 oz tomatoes
30 ml/2 tbsps olive oil
2.5 ml/½ tsp dried basil
2.5 ml/½ tsp dried oregano
150 ml/5 fl oz vegetable stock/water
100 g/4 oz cashew nuts
freshly ground black pepper

American
1 large onion
1 clove garlic, peeled and crushed
2 carrots
½ lb leeks
2 zucchini
¼ head cauliflower
½ lb tomatoes
2-3 tbsps olive oil
½ tsp dried basil
½ tsp dried oregano
½ cup vegetable stock/water
1 cup cashew nuts
freshly ground black pepper

Wash, trim and chop the vegetables. Heat the oil in a large heavy-bottomed pan and sauté the onion and garlic for 10 minutes. Add the remaining vegetables, the herbs and stock. Bring to the boil. Simmer gently until the vegetables are tender. Boil briskly, uncovered to reduce excess liquid if necessary. Toss in the cashew nuts and season to taste with black pepper.

Serve with potatoes, pasta, rice or wholewheat bread.

Ratatouille

It is difficult to make a first class ratatouille away from the sun drenched coast of the Mediterranean. The main problem is finding a good tomato, one which has been ripened slowly under a hot sun and is full of colour and flavour. All too often, here in Britain at least, the tomatoes are pale imitations of the real thing and it would seem as if they are grown more for uniformity of size than any culinary qualities. The large, ridged beefsteak tomato seems to be the nearest equivalent to the large, misshapen blood red tomato found in the markets of southern France but even so they must be ripe. If beefsteaks are unavailable or ridiculously expensive and it is too early or late for good, local grown tomatoes you may find it necessary to add a little tomato purée to the ratatouille to bolster up the flavour. This applies equally to other dishes in which the flavour of the tomato is a significant feature.

Metric/Imperial	American
1 aubergine	1 eggplant
225 g/8 oz courgettes	½ lb zucchini
1 green pepper	1 green pepper
225 g/8 oz mild onions	½ lb mild onions
2 beefsteak tomatoes	2 beefsteak tomatoes
30-45 ml/2-3 tbsps olive oil	3-4 tbsps olive oil
1 clove garlic, peeled and crushed	1 clove garlic, peeled and crushed
30 ml/2 tbsps fresh thyme, chopped	2-3 tbsps fresh thyme, chopped
1 bay leaf	1 bay leaf
15 ml/1 tbsp dry white wine	1½ tbsps dry white wine

Cut the aubergine and courgettes in half lengthways and slice 0.75 cm/¼ inch thick. Slice the pepper, onion and tomatoes.

Heat the olive oil in a large, heavy pan and sauté the onion and garlic until soft, being careful not to brown them. Add the pepper and cook for 5 minutes more. Then add the aubergines, followed by the courgettes and finally the tomatoes, frying each for a few minutes before adding the next vegetable. Stir the herbs into the ratatouille and pour over the wine. Season with black pepper and cover with a lid. Simmer over a low heat for 30-40 minutes until the vegetables are soft.

Serve with baked potatoes or wholewheat rolls.

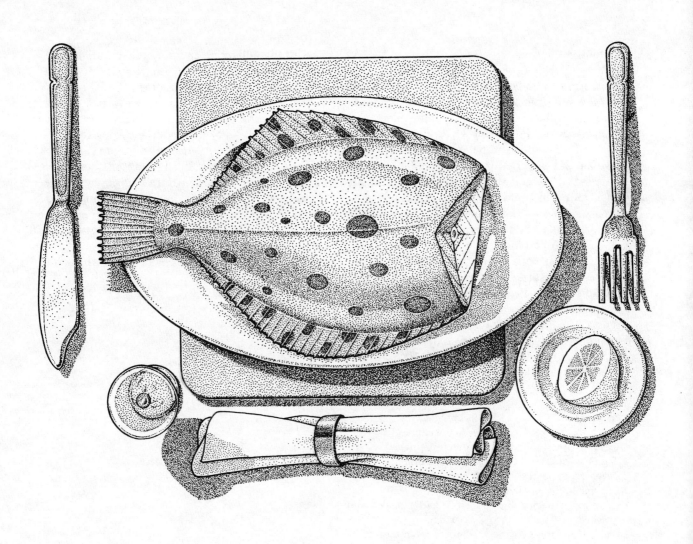

Fish

Cod in Tomato Sauce

Metric/Imperial	American
30 ml/2 tbsps olive oil	2-3 tbsps olive oil
450 g/1 lb ripe tomatoes, chopped	1 lb ripe tomatoes, chopped
1 clove garlic, peeled and crushed	1 clove garlic, peeled and crushed
15 ml/1 tbsp fresh parsley, chopped	1-1½ tbsps fresh parsley, chopped
60 ml/4 tbsps dry white wine	5-6 tbsps dry white wine
freshly ground black pepper	freshly ground black pepper
4 cod steaks	4 cod steaks

Heat the oil in a pan and sauté the tomatoes and garlic for 5 minutes. Add the parsley and wine and simmer for 8-10 minutes. Season to taste with black pepper. Liquidise until smooth. Pour half the sauce into a shallow ovenproof dish and arrange the cod steaks on top. Cover with the remaining sauce and a tight fitting lid.

Bake in a preheated oven, gas mark 5 (375°F/190°C) for 20-25 minutes.

Serve with potatoes and a green vegetable.

Haddock with Dill Seeds

Metric/Imperial	American
a good knob of unsalted butter	a good knob of sweet butter
1 onion, sliced	1 onion, sliced
2 leeks, sliced	2 leeks, sliced
4 carrots, thinly sliced	4 carrots, thinly sliced
75 ml/2½ fl oz dry white wine	¼ cup dry white wine
75 ml/2½ fl oz water	¼ cup water
2.5-5 ml/½-1 tsp dill seeds	½-1 tsp dill seeds
450 g/1 lb haddock fillets	1 lb haddock fillets

Melt the butter in a heavy-bottomed pan and sauté the onion for 10 minutes until soft. Add the remaining vegetables, the wine, water and dill seeds and cover with a tight fitting lid. Simmer gently until tender. Roughly chop the haddock, removing any skin and bones and add to the pan. Cook for a further 5-10 minutes.

It is delicious served with new potatoes.

Whiting Breton

This is a classic recipe and can be used with most types of fish, e.g. mackerel, sole, salmon and trout.

Metric/Imperial	American
4 small whiting	4 small whiting
wholewheat flour for dusting	wholewheat flour for dusting
freshly ground black pepper	freshly ground black pepper
50 g/2 oz unsalted butter	¼ cup sweet butter
juice of 1 lemon	juice of 1 lemon

Clean and gut the fish. Remove the head, open up the fish and place skin uppermost on a board. Press down along the backbone. Turn over and carefully remove the bones; they should come away quite easily. Dust the fish with a little flour and black pepper.

Melt the butter in a large pan and as soon as it begins to foam put in the fish, skins uppermost. Cook for 2-3 minutes before turning them over. Reduce the heat, cover with a lid and cook gently for 10-15 minutes. Squeeze the lemon juice over immediately before serving.

If the butter has blackened during cooking, drain it off and pour over a little freshly melted butter before adding the lemon juice.

Beurre Blanc

Metric/Imperial	American
3 shallots, finely chopped (or spring onions)	3 shallots, finely chopped (or scallions)
30 ml/2 tbsps white wine vinegar	2-3 tbsps white wine vinegar
30 ml/2 tbsps dry white wine	2-3 tbsps dry white wine
100-175 g/4-6 oz unsalted butter	½-¾ cup sweet butter

Place the shallots, the vinegar and wine in a small saucepan. Bring to the boil and cook until the shallots are soft and only 15-30 ml/1-2 tbsps of liquid remains. Remove from the heat and leave to cool. Cut the butter into small pieces. Return the pan to a very low heat and stir in the butter, a little at a time, until the sauce is smooth and creamy. Pour over the fish and serve immediately.

Grilled Red Mullet

Red mullet has been described as one of the finest fish in the sea but unfortunately few people get the opportunity to put its reputation to the test as it is a rare visitor to British fish stalls. It is also known as the Sea Woodcock because the fish's liver gives it a 'gamey' flavour and this organ should not be removed during gutting. For those unfamiliar with the internal layout of the red mullet's gut here is a passage from George Lassalle's book 'The Adventurous Fish Cook' which will help you to identify this vital organ.

'This (the liver) can be located near the thickest complex of blood vessels (the heart) of the fish, partially surrounding the intestine at the front end of the fish. The intestine should be removed and discarded, if possible without disturbing the liver'.

Grilling and cooking 'en papillote' are excellent methods of preparing this fish. Both preserve the delicate rosy pink colour of the skin and its friendly face!

To grill a red mullet, first remove its scales. Always scale a fish from the tail to the head, using a bluntish knife. I do this under running water in an effort to stop the scales flying off in all directions. Gut the fish (retaining the liver) and remove the gills. Wash and dry thoroughly but carefully.

Make several diagonal cuts on both sides of the fish and brush with olive oil. Lightly dust with black pepper and place on a sheet of foil. The foil not only collects the tasty juices that drip from the cooking fish but also makes the task of cleaning the grill that much easier. Grill on both sides.

Serve with a little lemon juice and melted butter or with beurre blanc.

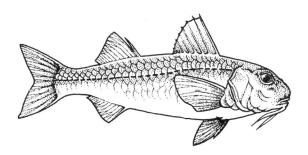

Scarborough Pie

Metric/Imperial
rough puff pastry:
175 g/6 oz unsalted butter
225 g/8 oz wholewheat
   flour
120 ml/8 tbsps cold water

Filling:
450 g/1 lb cod fillets
100 g/4 oz mussels, pre-
   pared and chopped
grated rind of 1 orange
good pinch of ground mace
freshly ground black
   pepper

To glaze:
a little milk

American
rough puff pastry:
¾ cup sweet butter
1½ cups wholewheat flour
10-12 tbsps cold water

Filling:
1 lb cod fillets
¼ lb mussels, prepared and
   chopped
grated rind of 1 orange
good pinch of ground mace
freshly ground black
   pepper

To glaze:
a little milk

To make the rough puff pastry chill the butter until very firm. Cut into small pieces and toss into a bowl containing the flour. Mix in the water, adding a little at a time until the mixture just begins to hold together — it may not be necessary to use all the water. Wrap in cling film and chill in a refrigerator for 15 minutes. Roll out on a floured board to form a rectangle. Fold over in thirds and press the edges together to seal. Chill for another 15 minutes. Repeat the rolling, folding and chilling three more times. The pastry is now ready. Chill until needed.

To make the filling put the fish in a pan and barely cover with water. Poach for 5-6 minutes. Drain and reserve the stock. Remove any skin and bones from the cooked cod and break into flakes.

Place in a buttered pie dish. Sprinkle the mussels over the top and season with the grated orange rind, mace and black pepper. Pour over 150 ml/5 fl oz (½ cup) fish stock.

Roll out the pastry and cover the pie. Brush with a little milk and bake in a preheated oven, gas mark 6 (400°F/200°C) for 25 minutes.

Serve with potatoes and stuffed onions.

Mackerel with Maitre d'Hotel Butter

This simple but delicious sauce can be served with almost any type of fish.

Metric/Imperial
4 small mackerel
a little olive oil
50 g/2 oz unsalted butter
juice of 1 lemon
fresh parsley, finely
   chopped

American
4 small mackerel
a little olive oil
¼ cup sweet butter
juice of 1 lemon
fresh parsley, finely
   chopped

Clean and gut the fish. Brush them with a little olive oil and place under a hot grill. Turn once to cook the other side. When cooked place them on a warm serving dish. Meanwhile melt the butter in a small saucepan. Add the lemon juice and parsley. Pour the sauce over the fish and serve immediately.

Herrings with Devilled Onions

Metric/Imperial
4 herrings
wholewheat flour for
   dusting
freshly ground black
   pepper
a little sesame oil
1 onion, chopped
10 ml/2 tsps Dijon mustard
150 ml/5 fl oz water
2.5 ml/½ tsp white wine
   vinegar

American
4 herrings
wholewheat flour for
   dusting
freshly ground black
   pepper
a little sesame oil
1 onion, chopped
2 tsps Dijon mustard
½ cup water
½ tsp white wine vinegar

Clean and gut the fish. Wipe dry and dust with flour and black pepper. Heat a little sesame oil in a frying pan and cook the herrings for 7-8 minutes, turning once until tender.

Meanwhile in another pan heat a little more oil and sauté the onions until golden brown. Stir in the mustard and pour over the water and vinegar. Bring to the boil and reduce slightly. Pour over the fish and serve immediately.

Matelote d'Aiguille (Garfish in Wine)

Garfish is becoming an increasingly common sight
on the fishmonger's slab. It is easily recognised,
being one of the most elegant and unusual-looking
fish. At the end of its long, slender body is a 10
cm/2 inch 'beak' complete with tiny teeth. The
flesh is firm, white and pleasantly flavoured and
looks extremely attractive against the fish's electric-
blue bones. The bones really have to be seen to be
believed. I try to make a feature of them when
serving a dish of garfish. Try cutting the fish into
steaks before cooking and then just before serving
open each segment down the back to expose the
bones. A fiddly job but well worth the effort.

Metric/Imperial	American
675-900 g/1½-2 lbs garfish	1½-2 lbs garfish
25 g/1 oz unsalted butter	2-3 tbsps sweet butter
2 onions, chopped	2 onions, chopped
2 leeks, chopped	2 leeks, chopped
275 ml/10 fl oz dry white wine	1¼ cups dry white wine
275 ml/10 fl oz court-bouillon	1¼ cups court-bouillon
50 g/2 oz unsalted butter	¼ cup sweet butter
25 g/1 oz unbleached white flour	1½ tbsps unbleached white all-purpose flour
freshly ground black pepper	freshly ground black pepper
a little fresh parsley, chopped	a little fresh parsley, chopped

Gut the fish and remove both head and tail.
Wash and dry carefully. Cut into 5 cm/2 inch
steaks. Melt 25 g/1 oz (2-3 tbsps) butter in a large
pan and lightly fry the onions and leeks until soft,
being careful not to brown. Lay the fish steaks on
top of the sautéed vegetables and pour over the
wine and court-bouillon. Poach for 5-8 minutes.
When cooked, remove the fish and vegetables and
place on a warm serving dish. Pour over 15-30
ml/2-3 tbsps of stock, cover and keep warm.

Knead the remaining butter and flour together
to form a smooth, stiff paste. Shape into small
balls. Bring the fish stock to the boil and gradually
add the butter balls. Boil for 4-5 minutes, stirring
constantly until the sauce thickens. Season with a
little black pepper. Pour the sauce over a bowl of
cooked brown rice and serve with the fish.

Braised green peas with butter go well with this
dish.

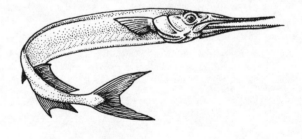

Trout with Hazel Nut Stuffing

Metric/Imperial
4 small trout
a little olive oil
40 g/1½ oz unsalted butter
175 g/6 oz button mush-
  rooms, finely chopped
1 clove garlic, peeled and
  crushed
100 g/4 oz hazel nuts,
  ground
juice of 1 lemon
freshly ground black
  pepper

American
4 small trout
a little olive oil
2-3 tbsps sweet butter
1½ cups finely chopped
  button mushrooms
1 clove garlic, peeled and
  crushed
1 cup ground hazel nuts
juice of 1 lemon
freshly ground black
  pepper

Clean and gut the fish. Brush their skins with a little olive oil and place them in a shallow ovenproof dish. To make the stuffing, melt the butter in a small pan and gently cook the mushrooms and garlic for 3-4 minutes. Add the ground nuts, 60-75 ml/4-5 tbsps olive oil and the lemon juice. Mix together well and season with black pepper.

Stuff the filling into the trout and bake in a moderate oven, gas mark 4 (350°F/180°C) for 15-20 minutes.

Serve with new potatoes and Salade de Ventoux.

Trout with Sesame Seeds

Metric/Imperial
25 g/1 oz unsalted butter
30 ml/2 tbsps sesame oil
4 small trout, cleaned and
  gutted
25 g/1 oz sesame seeds,
  lightly roasted
45 ml/3 tbsps lemon juice
30 ml/2 tbsps red wine
45 ml/3 tbsps fish
  stock/water

American
2-3 tbsps sweet butter
2-3 tbsps sesame oil
4 small trout, cleaned and
  gutted
¼ cup sesame seeds, lightly
  roasted
3-4 tbsps lemon juice
2-3 tbsps red wine
3-4 tbsps fish stock/water

Heat the butter and oil in a large frying pan. Add the trout and cook gently, turning once. When almost cooked, add the sesame seeds and lemon juice. Baste the fish until tender. Remove from the pan and place on a serving dish. Keep in a warm place. Pour the red wine into the pan and add the stock/water. Heat through. Pour over the fish and serve.

I like to serve trout on a bed of sautéed mushrooms.

Whitebait

Whitebait are the small fry or young of herrings and sprats. Slender, silvery grey and measuring no more than 3-4 cm/1½ inches long they are generally deep-fried and eaten whole. There is no need to gut or clean whitebait, simply give them a good rinse under running water. However, be wary of the slightly larger sprat which is often to be found masquerading in the place of its tiny offspring. The bones and head of sprats are more developed and the experience of eating them whole can be, to put it mildly, a little crunchy and not to everyone's liking.

Fresh whitebait have long been one of the treats of early summer. They freeze very well and can now be bought throughout the year in small frozen rectangular blocks. Allow 100 g/4 oz per person.

To cook whitebait dip them in milk and then shake in a paper bag containing a little wholewheat flour. Shake off any surplus flour before deep frying in oil. When cooked they should be so crisp that they actually rustle as one piles them onto the plate.

Serve immediately with slices of brown bread and butter, lemon juice and freshly ground black pepper.

Fish Cakes

Makes 10-12

Metric/Imperial	American
350 g/12 oz white fish (cod or haddock)	¾ lb white fish (cod or haddock)
350 g/12 oz potatoes, cooked and mashed	¾ lb potatoes, cooked and mashed
grated rind of 1 lemon	grated rind of 1 lemon
45 ml/3 tbsps fresh parsley, chopped	3-4 tbsps fresh parsley, chopped
freshly ground black pepper	freshly ground black pepper
a little fish stock/milk	a little fish stock/milk
50 g/2 oz medium oatmeal	¼ cup medium oatmeal
oil for frying	oil for frying

Cook the fish and remove the bones and skin. Mix the fish, potatoes, grated lemon rind and parsley together. Season to taste with black pepper. Add a little stock or milk if the mixture is too dry.

Shape into rounds, approximately 1.25 cm/½ inch thick. A biscuit cutter is very useful for this. Coat in oatmeal and shallow fry until golden brown on both sides.

Spicy Fish Cakes

Makes 16-18

Metric/Imperial	American
1 onion	1 onion
2 green chillies	2 green chilies
2 cloves garlic, peeled	2 cloves garlic, peeled
30 ml/2 tbsps sunflower oil	2-3 tbsps sunflower oil
5 ml/1 tsp turmeric	1 tsp turmeric
5 ml/1 tsp ground coriander	1 tsp ground coriander
5 ml/1 tsp cumin seeds	1 tsp cumin seeds
5 ml/1 tsp black mustard seeds	1 tsp black mustard seeds
450 g/1 lb white fish, cooked and filleted (haddock, cod, whiting etc.)	1 lb white fish, cooked and filleted (haddock, cod, whiting etc.)
30 ml/2 tbsps fresh coriander, finely chopped	2-3 tbsps fresh coriander, finely chopped
10 ml/2 tsps lemon juice	2 tsps lemon juice
freshly ground black pepper	freshly ground black pepper
450 g/1 lb potatoes, cooked and mashed	1 lb potatoes, cooked and mashed
2 eggs beaten	2 eggs, beaten
100 g/4 oz soft wholewheat breadcrumbs	1 cup soft wholewheat breadcrumbs
oil for deep frying	oil for deep frying

Finely chop the onion, chillies and garlic and fry in the sunflower oil until soft. Stir in the spices and cook for 2-3 minutes. Break the fish into large flakes and add to the pan with the fresh coriander and lemon juice. Season with black pepper. Mix in the potatoes, taking care to retain some of the fish's texture.

Form into small balls (approx 2.5 cm/1 inch in diameter). Dip in beaten egg and coat with breadcrumbs. Deep fry in hot oil until golden brown. Drain on absorbent paper.

Serve with a vegetable curry and brown rice.

Fresh Salmon Pâté

Metric/Imperial
225 g/8 oz salmon,
   poached
   in court-bouillon
100 g/4 oz unsalted butter
15 ml/1 tbsp fresh parsley,
   chopped
1 clove garlic, peeled and
   crushed
pinch cayenne pepper
grated rind of 1 lemon
15 ml/1 tbsp lemon juice
45 ml/3 tbsp fish stock
freshly ground black
   pepper

American
½ lb salmon, poached in
   court-bouillon
½ cup sweet butter
1½ tbsps fresh parsley,
   chopped
1 clove garlic, peeled and
   crushed
pinch cayenne pepper
grated rind of 1 lemon
1½ tbsps lemon juice
3-4 tbsps fish stock
freshly ground black
   pepper

Remove the skin and bones from the fish. Cream the butter and pound with the fish, parsley and garlic until smooth. Add the remaining ingredients and mix together well. Adjust seasoning to taste. Spoon into a pot and chill.

If the pâté is not to be used within 12 hours seal the top with melted butter.

Serve with slices of brown bread and lemon wedges.

Octopus

The slippery mass of tentacles seen at the fishmonger's is not a very appetising sight and it is hardly surprising that so few people appreciate the gastronomic value of octopus. Yet underneath the ugly exterior is a milky-white flesh that has a firm, slightly chewy texture and an excellent flavour.

In an attempt to make their wares more attractive fishmongers display their octopuses in different ways. Some rely on their customers' sound judgement and display them whole, in all their glory, while others only sell the tentacles. My local fishmonger has struck a pleasing balance for he simply removes the grey-blue skin revealing the more appetising white meat.

Octopuses vary in size but it is worth remembering that the larger the specimen the longer it will take to cook. With very large octopuses only the tentacles are worth eating and even then I suggest that you beat them well with a rolling pin until they lose their resilience. The most tender, succulent flesh is found in those octopus which are less than 37.5 cm (15 inches) long. Very small ones with tentacles less than 10 cm (4 inches) long can be cooked whole.

One of the main problems facing a novice cook is knowing how to prepare an octopus for the pot, for the instructions given in many cookery books are totally inadequate. They usually state, 'remove the beak, eyes and internal organs' and I well remember when I tackled my first octopus it took me at least five minutes to locate the eyes and if I actually removed the beak it was through luck rather than skill.

I must admit that preparing an octopus is not

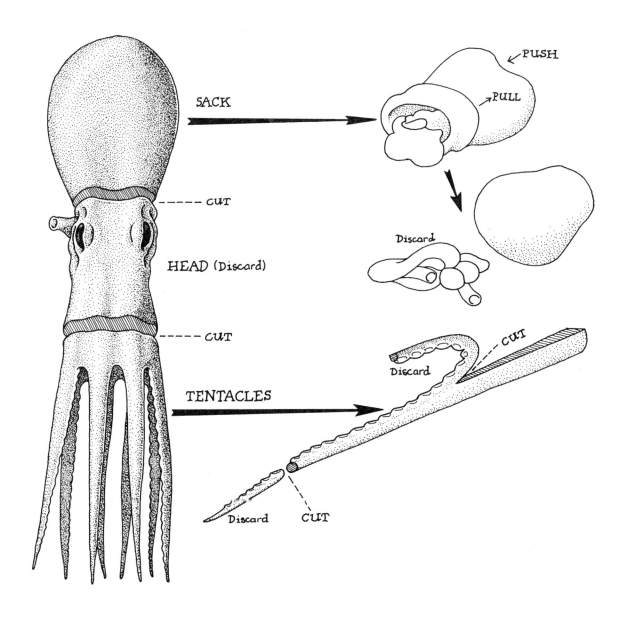

one of my favourite pastimes but I have a simple method that is quick, straightforward and relatively clean.

First identify the tentacles, the sac-like body and the narrow head running between the two. Remove the head by cutting off the tentacles and the sac-like body and discard it.

Cut the suckers and any loose skin from the tentacles. Ease the body inside out, cutting the inners away from the fleshy bag as you do so. Rinse the empty sac-like body and the tentacles under cold running water. Pull away the remaining dark skin, blanching it if it proves stubborn. The octopus bag and tentacles are now ready for cooking.

Mediterranean Octopus Stew

Metric/Imperial	American
2 octopuses (weighing ½ kg/1-1¼ lbs each)	2 octopuses (weighing 1-1¼ lbs each)
120 ml/8 tbsps olive oil	a scant ½ cup olive oil
4 cloves garlic, peeled and crushed	4 cloves garlic, peeled and crushed
4 sticks celery, chopped	4 sticks celery, chopped
4 carrots, diced	4 carrots, diced
4 potatoes, diced	4 potatoes, diced
45 ml/3 tbsps tomato purée	3-4 tbsps tomato purée
30 ml/2 tbsps white wine vinegar	2-3 tbsps white wine vinegar
juice of 1 lemon	juice of 1 lemon
575 ml/1 pint water	2½ cups water
freshly ground black pepper	freshly ground black pepper
2 sprigs fresh rosemary	2 sprigs fresh rosemary

Clean and prepare each octopus as described on the previous page. Cut into small pieces.

Heat the oil in a large pan and fry the octopus for 5 minutes. Add the vegetables and sauté for a further 5 minutes. Add the remaining ingredients, cover and simmer for 45-60 minutes until the octopus is tender.

Serve with a crusty loaf.

Octopus with Saffron Rice

Metric/Imperial	American
2 octopuses (weighing ½ kg/1-1¼ lbs each)	2 octopuses (weighing 1-1¼ lbs each)
60 ml/4 tbsps olive oil	5-6 tbsps olive oil
2 onions, sliced	2 onions, sliced
2 cloves garlic, peeled and crushed	2 cloves garlic, peeled and crushed
juice of 2 limes	juice of 2 limes
45 ml/3 tbsps fresh parsley, chopped	3-4 tbsps fresh parsley, chopped
freshly ground black pepper	freshly ground black pepper
425 ml/15 fl oz water	1¾ cups water
350 g/12 oz long grain brown rice	2 cups long grain brown rice
a good pinch saffron	a good pinch saffron

Clean and prepare the octopus as described on page 86.

Heat the oil in a large, heavy pan and fry the octopus, onion and garlic for 5-8 minutes. Add the lime juice, parsley and water. Season well with black pepper. Cover and simmer for 45-60 minutes until the octopus is tender.

Meanwhile place the remaining ingredients in a pan with 850 ml/1½ pints (4 cups) water. Bring to the boil and simmer for 40 minutes. When all the water has been absorbed and the rice is soft remove from the heat. Leave to stand, covered, for 5 minutes.

Serve the octopus on a bed of saffron rice.

Meat, Poultry and Game

Lamb with Herbs

Metric/Imperial
900 g/2 lbs lamb (leg,
 breast or neck)
150 ml/5 fl oz stock
sprig of fresh rosemary
1 bay leaf
freshly ground black
 pepper

American
2 lbs lamb (leg, breast,
 or neck)
½ cup stock
sprig of fresh rosemary
1 bay leaf
freshly ground black
 pepper

Grease a baking tin just large enough to hold the meat. Place the rosemary and bay leaf in the bottom. Arrange the lamb on top and sprinkle with black pepper. Pour over the stock and cover with foil. Bake in a preheated oven, gas mark 7 (425°F/220°C) for 45-60 minutes. Remove the foil and brown the meat. Skim off the fat and remove the herbs before serving.

Serve with potatoes en papillotes and stir-fried vegetable medley.

Lamb in Cider

Metric/Imperial
1½ kg/3 lb joint of lamb
2 sprigs of fresh rosemary
freshly ground black
 pepper
5 ml/1 tsp ground ginger
10 ml/2 tsps clear honey
275 ml/10 fl oz cider

American
3 lb joint of lamb
2 sprigs of fresh rosemary
freshly ground black
 pepper
1 tsp ground ginger
2 tsps clear honey
1¼ cups cider

Put the lamb and rosemary in a roasting tin and season with black pepper. Sprinkle with ground ginger and dribble the honey over the top. Pour the cider around the meat.

Roast in a preheated oven, gas mark 7 (425°F/220°C) for ½ hour. Reduce the temperature to gas mark 4 (350°F/180°C) and cook for 1½-2 hours, basting frequently. Make a gravy with the cooking liquid and serve.

Serve with rice balls.

Lamb Chops in Spicy Tomato Sauce

Metric/Imperial
15 ml/1 tbsp olive oil
25 g/1 oz unsalted butter
8 lamb chops, with fat
  trimmed off

American
1-1½ tbsps olive oil
2-3 tbsps sweet butter
8 lamb chops, with fat
  trimmed off

Sauce:
60 ml/4 tbsps olive oil
1 onion, finely chopped
2 cloves garlic, peeled and
  crushed
5 ml/1 tsp black mustard
  seeds
10 ml/ 2 tsps cumin seeds
1.25 ml/¼ tsp cayenne
  pepper
1.25 ml/¼ tsp garam
  masala
450 g/1 lb ripe tomatoes

Sauce:
5-6 tbsps olive oil
1 onion, finely chopped
2 cloves garlic, peeled and
  crushed
1 tsp black mustard seeds
2 tsps cumin seeds
¼ tsp cayenne pepper
¼ tsp garam masala
1 lb ripe tomatoes

Heat the oil and butter in a pan and fry the chops until well browned on both sides. Keep warm while preparing the sauce.

To make the sauce heat the oil in a pan and add the onion and garlic. Fry until golden brown and soft. Add the spices and sauté for a further 1-2 minutes. Chop the tomatoes and mix with the other ingredients in the pan. Bring to the boil, cover and simmer for 15 minutes.

Meanwhile preheat the oven to gas mark 4 (350°F/180°C). Place the chops in a baking dish and pour the sauce over the top. Bake for 45-60 minutes until the chops are tender.

Serve with baked potatoes and cauliflower.

Liver and Onion Casserole

This recipe comes from one of my grandmother's cookery books. In spite of following these instructions to the letter, neither my mother nor I have been able to make a liver and onion casserole taste quite as good as she did.

Metric/Imperial
450 g/1 lb lamb's liver
flour for dusting
25 g/1 oz unsalted butter
100 g/4 oz soft wholewheat
  breadcrumbs
10 ml/2 tsps mustard
  powder
good pinch dried sage
3 onions, sliced
freshly ground black
  pepper
275 ml/10 fl oz stock

American
1 lb lamb's liver
flour for dusting
2-3 tbsps sweet butter
1 cup soft wholewheat
  breadcrumbs
2 tsps mustard powder
good pinch dried sage
3 onions, sliced
freshly ground black
  pepper
1¼ cups stock

To garnish:
fresh parsley, chopped

To garnish:
fresh parsley, chopped

Dust the liver in flour, shake well to remove any surplus. Melt the butter in a pan and add the liver. Brown quickly on both sides being careful not to over cook it.

Mix the breadcrumbs, mustard powder and sage together in a bowl. Place a layer of liver in the bottom of an ovenproof dish and cover with a layer of breadcrumbs and follow with a layer of onions. Repeat the three layers, sprinkling black pepper between each one. Finish with a layer of breadcrumbs. Pour in the stock and cover. Bake in a preheated oven, gas mark 4 (350°F/180°C) for 45 minutes.

Sprinkle with parsley before serving.

Faggots

Metric/Imperial	American
225 g/½ lb pig's liver	½ lb pig's liver
225 g/½ lb fat bacon	½ lb fat bacon
1 large onion	1 large onion
225 g/½ lb stale wholewheat bread	½ lb stale wholewheat bread
225 g/½ lb medium oatmeal	½ lb medium oatmeal
2.5 ml/½ tsp dried mixed herbs	½ tsp dried mixed herbs
a good pinch dried sage	a good pinch dried sage
2 eggs, beaten	2 eggs, beaten
milk if necessary	milk if necessary

Mince the liver, bacon, onion and bread and place in a mixing bowl. Add the oatmeal, herbs and beaten eggs. The mixture should be fairly moist, add a little milk if necessary. Shape into squares and place on a baking tray. Cook in a preheated oven, gas mark 4 (350°F/180°C) for about 1 hour.

Serve hot with gravy, potatoes and vegetables.

Spiced Beef Burgers

Metric/Imperial	American
450 g/1 lb minced beef	1 lb minced beef
1 onion, grated	1 onion, grated
freshly ground black pepper	freshly ground black pepper
5 ml/1 tsp ground coriander	1 tsp ground coriander
5 ml/1 tsp ground cumin	1 tsp ground cumin
pinch chilli powder	pinch chili powder
45 ml/3 tbsps fresh coriander, chopped	3-4 tbsps fresh coriander, chopped
oil for frying	oil for frying

Mix all the ingredients together and shape into burgers. Fry, grill or barbecue until evenly brown and cooked through.

Serve with bread rolls and a tomato and onion salad.

Beef Stew

Metric/Imperial	American
675 g/1½ lbs stewing beef	1½ lbs stewing beef
flour for dusting	flour for dusting
45 ml/3 tbsps sunflower oil	3-4 tbsps sunflower oil
2 onions, chopped	2 onions, chopped
575 ml/1 pint stock	2½ cups stock
1 stick celery, sliced	1 stick celery, sliced
2 carrots, chopped	2 carrots, chopped
sprig of fresh thyme	sprig of fresh thyme
sprig of fresh parsley	sprig of fresh parsley
sprig of fresh sage	sprig of fresh sage
1 bay leaf	1 bay leaf
freshly ground black pepper	freshly ground black pepper

Cut the meat into chunks and coat in flour. Heat the oil in a pan and fry the meat and onions until lightly browned. Place in an ovenproof dish. Add 15 ml/1 tbsp flour to the pan and cook for 1-2 minutes, stirring frequently. Pour in the stock and stir until it begins to thicken. Place all the remaining ingredients in the dish and pour over the 'gravy'. Season with black pepper. Cover with a lid.

Bake in a preheated oven, gas mark 3 (325°F/170°C) for about 2 hours until the meat is tender.

Stir-Fried Chicken with Mange-Touts

Metric/Imperial	American
the wings and legs of 1 cooked chicken	the wings and legs of 1 cooked chicken
15 ml/1 tbsp sesame oil	1-1½ tbsps sesame oil
5 cm/2 inch fresh root ginger, peeled and grated	2 inch fresh ginger root, peeled and grated
1 yellow pepper, sliced	1 yellow pepper, sliced
100 g/4 oz French beans	¼ lb snap beans
100 g/4 oz mange-touts	¼ lb mange-touts
juice of 1 lemon	juice of 1 lemon
freshly ground black pepper	freshly ground black pepper

Remove the flesh from the chicken and cut into bite-sized pieces. Heat the sesame oil in a wok and toss in the ginger and vegetables. Stir-fry for 2-3 minutes. Add the chicken and fry for 5 minutes more. Pour over the lemon juice and season with black pepper. Serve immediately.

Serve with brown rice, buckwheat spaghetti or new potatoes. .

Chicken with Spanish Rice

Metric/Imperial
1½ kg/3 lb roasting
  chicken, oven-ready
60 ml/4 tbsps olive oil
freshly ground black
  pepper
3 cloves garlic, peeled
1 lemon

the rice:
15 ml/1 tbsp olive oil
1 onion, sliced
225 g/8 oz long grain
  brown rice
275 ml/10 fl oz chicken
  stock/water
275 ml/10 fl oz dry white
  wine
a good pinch saffron
100 g/4 oz raisins
100 g/4 oz blanched
  almonds, halved and
  lightly roasted

American
3 lb roasting chicken, oven-
  ready
5-6 tbsps olive oil
freshly ground black
  pepper
3 cloves garlic, peeled
1 lemon

the rice:
1-1½ tbsps olive oil
1 onion, sliced
1¼ cups long grain brown
  rice
1¼ cups chicken stock/
  water
1¼ cups dry white wine
a good pinch saffron
¾ cup raisins
1 cup blanched almonds,
  halved and lightly
  roasted

Rub the chicken with the olive oil and place in a roasting tin. Sprinkle with black pepper and pour over the juice of 1 lemon. Place the garlic, half a squeezed lemon and 15 ml/1 tbsp of olive oil inside the bird. Bake in a preheated oven, gas mark 5 (375°F/190°C) for 1 hour, basting frequently.

Meanwhile heat the remaining oil in a heavy pan and sauté the onion lightly for 10-15 minutes. Stir in the rice until it is well coated in oil. Pour over the stock and wine and add the saffron, raisins and almonds. Bring to the boil and simmer for 35-40 minutes until the rice is tender and dry.

Drain the cooking fat and juice from the roasting tin. Strain off the fat and stir the rich, brown chicken juices into the cooked rice. Place the cooked chicken in the centre of a large serving plate and spoon the rice around.

Serve with Joseph's technicolour salad.

Chicken Curry

Metric/Imperial
45 ml/3 tbsps groundnut oil
2.5 cm/1 inch fresh root ginger, peeled and grated
1 green chilli, chopped
2 cloves garlic, peeled and crushed
2 onions, chopped
10 ml/2 tsps ground cumin
10 ml/2 tsps ground coriander
5 ml/1 tsp turmeric
2.5 ml/½ tsp ground cardamom
1½ kg/3 lb chicken, jointed
50 g/2 oz creamed coconut, grated
350 ml/12 fl oz boiling water
juice of 1 lemon
30 ml/2 tbsps fresh coriander, chopped

American
3-4 tbsps peanut oil
1 inch fresh ginger root, peeled and grated
1 green chili, chopped
2 cloves garlic, peeled and crushed
2 onions, chopped
2 tsps ground cumin
2 tsps ground coriander
1 tsp turmeric
½ tsp ground cardamom
3 lb chicken, jointed
¼ cup creamed coconut, grated
a scant 1½ cups boiling water
juice of 1 lemon
2-3 tbsps fresh coriander, chopped

Heat the oil in a large pan. Gently fry the ginger, chilli, garlic and onion for 10 minutes. Add the spices and cook for further 1-2 minutes, stirring frequently. Add the chicken joints and fry, turning occasionally, until well coated in oil and spices.

Dissolve the coconut in the boiling water before pouring over the chicken. Bring to the boil, cover and simmer for 1-1½ hours until the chicken is tender. Season with lemon juice and sprinkle with fresh coriander before serving.

Serve with rice or chapati.

Roast Duckling

The term duckling generally applies to birds less than six months old. Although young birds are generally more tender than older ones it is a mistake to buy too young a bird as they may have little flesh on their bones.

Ducks, whatever their age, have a shallow breast which can make carving something of a problem. Also, they are all well endowed with fat. So much so that one of the chief preoccupations when cooking a bird is to release and drain off as much fat as possible before it reaches the table.

Although not as economical or as easy to prepare as chicken, for instance, duckling is succulent, tender and full of flavour and makes an excellent roast.

Metric/Imperial	American
2.2 kg/5 lb duckling, oven-ready	5 lb duckling, oven-ready
Stock:	Stock:
giblets	giblets
1 onion, chopped	1 onion, chopped
1 carrot, chopped	1 carrot, chopped
1 stick celery, chopped	1 stick celery, chopped
575 ml/1 pint water	2½ cups water
1 lemon, chopped	1 lemon, chopped
large bunch fresh thyme	large bunch fresh thyme
large bunch fresh marjoram	large bunch fresh marjoram
15 ml/1 tbsp wholewheat flour	1-1½ tbsps wholewheat flour
freshly ground black pepper	freshly ground black pepper

Place the giblets, vegetables, water, lemon and herbs in a large pan. Bring to the boil, skim and simmer for 1 hour. Strain.

Heat the oven to gas mark 7 (425°F/220°C). Put the duckling on a wire rack and stand over a baking tray. Prick the skin with a sharp fork or skewer. Cook for 15 minutes. Reduce the oven temperature to gas mark 4 (350°F/180°C) and cook for a further 45 minutes, basting occasionally.

Remove the duckling and the wire rack and drain off the excess fat that has collected in the baking tray. Stand the duckling in the baking tray and pour over 425 ml/15 fl oz (1¾ cups) stock. Return to the oven and cook for 40 minutes, basting every now and then. When tender place the bird on a serving dish. Remove the stock and strain off any surplus fat. Sprinkle the flour into the bottom of the baking tray and gradually stir in the stock. Season with black pepper. Serve with the bird.

Pigeon Pie

Pigeons seem to have fallen out of favour in Britain, with the result that many of our birds find their way onto European tables. This is a great pity because pigeon is relatively inexpensive and the meat has a fine, gamey flavour.

Unfortunately, every once in a while an aged bird slips through the net and finds its way into a shop. Although the meat smells and tastes as delicious as that of its younger relatives it can be extremely tough and few people have sufficient strength and determination to appreciate its gastronomic qualities.

Some books suggest that before selecting a pigeon for the pot the 'pigeon fancier' should study each bird's feet. If they are soft, supple and free from scales it can be assumed that the bird is reasonably young and tender. However, in my local area pigeons are generally sold oven-ready and one simply has to take pot luck. If in doubt about the age of a bird I suggest cooking it in a stew or pie rather than braising or roasting it.

Metric/Imperial

3 wood pigeons, oven ready

Stock:
1 onion
1 carrot
425 ml/15 fl oz water
1 glass red wine
1 bay leaf
a sprig of fresh thyme
a sprig of fresh parsley

Filling:
2 medium potatoes
2 onions
wholewheat flour for dusting
30 ml/2 tbsps sunflower oil
100 g/4 oz mushrooms, sliced
1 bay leaf
a sprig of fresh thyme
a sprig of fresh parsley
freshly ground black pepper

Pastry:
225 g/8 oz wholewheat flour
75 g/3 oz butter
30 ml/2 tbsps sunflower oil
40 ml/8 tsps cold water

American

3 wood pigeons, oven-ready

Stock:
1 onion
1 carrot
1¾ cups water
1 glass red wine
1 bay leaf
a sprig of fresh thyme
a sprig of fresh parsley

Filling:
2 medium potatoes
2 onions
wholewheat flour for dusting
2-3 tbsps sunflower oil
1 cup sliced mushrooms
1 bay leaf
a sprig of fresh thyme
a sprig of fresh parsley
freshly ground black pepper

Pastry:
1½ cups wholewheat flour
a scant ½ cup butter
2-3 tbsps sunflower oil
8 tsps cold water

Cut each bird into four pieces — two legs and two breasts. Remove the meat from each joint. To make the stock put the bones in a pan with the peeled and sliced onion and carrot, the water, wine and the herbs. Bring to the boil, skim and reduce to a simmer. Cover and cook for 1 hour.

To make the filling peel and chop the potatoes and onions. Cut the meat into chunks and dust with a little flour. Heat the oil in a pan and brown the meat evenly. Transfer to a pie dish. Sauté the onions in the remaining oil and add to the pie dish with the potatoes and mushrooms. Strain the stock and pour over the pie filling. Add the herbs and season with black pepper.

To make the pastry put the flour in a mixing bowl and rub in the butter and oil. Add the water and knead to form a pastry dough. Roll out on a floured board and cover the pie. For an attractive glaze brush with a little beaten egg.

Bake in a preheated oven, gas mark 7 (425°F/220°C) for 20 minutes. Reduce the temperature to gas mark 3 (325°F/170°C) and cook for a further 1½ hours. Cover the pastry with foil as soon as it is browned.

Serve with baked potatoes and carrots with thyme.

Rabbit Casserole

Metric/Imperial	*American*
1 rabbit, skinned, cleaned and jointed	1 rabbit, skinned, cleaned and jointed
wholewheat flour for dusting	wholewheat flour for dusting
45 ml/3 tbsps olive oil	3-4 tbsps olive oil
25 g/1 oz unsalted butter	2-3 tbsps sweet butter
12 pickling onions/shallots, peeled	12 pickling onions/shallots, peeled
1 clove garlic, peeled and crushed	1 clove garlic, peeled and crushed
1 carrot, chopped	1 carrot, chopped
1 leek, chopped	1 leek, chopped
1 glass red wine	1 glass red wine
275-425 ml/½-¾ pint stock/water	1¼-1¾ cups stock/water
sprig of fresh thyme	sprig of fresh thyme
sprig of fresh rosemary	sprig of fresh rosemary
sprig of fresh parsley	sprig of fresh parsley
1 bay leaf	1 bay leaf
freshly ground black pepper	freshly ground black pepper

Dust the rabbit with a little flour. Heat the oil and butter in a pan and brown the rabbit joints. Remove and sauté the onions and garlic until golden brown. Return the rabbit to the pan with the carrot and leek. Pour over the wine and add sufficient stock to barely cover the contents of the pan. Add the herbs and season with black pepper.

Cover and bring to the boil. Simmer gently until the meat is tender. This can take anything from 45 minutes to 2 hours depending on the age of the rabbit.

Serve with boiled potatoes and broccoli.

Devilled Rabbit

Metric/Imperial	*American*
1 rabbit, skinned, cleaned and jointed	1 rabbit, skinned, cleaned and jointed
wholewheat flour for dusting	wholewheat flour for dusting
30-45 ml/2-3 tbsps sunflower oil	2-4 tbsps sunflower oil
1 onion	1 onion
a few sprigs of fresh thyme	a few sprigs of fresh thyme
1 glass dry white wine	1 glass dry white wine
1-2 glasses chicken stock	1-2 glasses chicken stock
15 ml/1 tbsp Dijon mustard	1-1½ tbsps Dijon mustard
10 ml/2 tsps English mustard	2 tsps English mustard
freshly ground black pepper	freshly ground black pepper
30-45 ml/2-3 tbsps sour cream	3-4 tbsps sour cream

Dry the rabbit joints and dust them lightly with flour. Heat the oil in a pan and sauté the meat until lightly browned. Peel and slice the onion and add to the pan. Cook for a further 5 minutes. Add the thyme, wine and stock and half the mustard. Season liberally with black pepper. Bring to the boil and simmer, turning the meat occasionally until the rabbit is tender. A young rabbit will cook in just less than an hour but old, tough animals may take up to 2 hours.

Just before serving add the remaining mustard and stir in the sour cream.

Serve with wholewheat croûtons, boiled potatoes and a side salad.

Jugged Hare

Metric/Imperial
1 hare, skinned, cleaned
    and jointed

Marinade:
sprig of fresh thyme
sprig of fresh parsley
1 bay leaf
850 ml/1½ pints stock/
    water
2 glasses red wine

Remaining ingredients:
30 ml/2 tbsps sunflower oil
2 onions, chopped
2 carrots, chopped
100 g/4 oz mushrooms,
    sliced
pinch ground cloves
pinch ground cinnamon
pinch ground nutmeg
15 ml/1 tbsp beurre manié

American
1 hare, skinned, cleaned
    and jointed

Marinade:
sprig of fresh thyme
sprig of fresh parsley
1 bay leaf
3¼ cups stock/water
2 glasses red wine

Remaining ingredients:
2-3 tbsps sunflower oil
2 onions, chopped
2 carrots, chopped
1 cup sliced mushrooms
pinch ground cloves
pinch ground cinnamon
pinch ground nutmeg
1-1½ tbsps beurre manié

Place the hare and the marinade ingredients in a large container and leave in a cool place overnight. Drain and reserve the stock.

Heat the oil in a pan and fry the meat until well browned. Remove and sauté the onions and carrots in the same pan for 5 minutes. Add the meat, the mushrooms, the stock and spices. Cover and bake in a preheated oven gas mark 3 (325°F/170°C) for 1-1½ hours until the meat is tender.

Transfer the hare and vegetables to a hot serving dish and add the beurre manié to the gravy, a little at a time. Stir well and simmer gently until it begins to thicken. Pour the gravy over the meat and serve.

Serve with baked vegetables à la Provençale.

Beurre Manié is a mixture of flour and butter (in equal amounts) which are kneaded together until they form a smooth paste. It is used as a thickening agent.

Stocks, Sauces and Salad Dressings

STOCKS

Beef Stock

Ideal for gravies, stews and all meat dishes.

Metric/Imperial	American
1.5 kg/3 lbs beef bones, chopped	3 lbs beef bones, chopped
225 g/8 oz shin beef	½ lb shin beef
2½ litres/4 pints water	10 cups water
2 onions	2 onions
2 leeks	2 leeks
2 carrots	2 carrots
sprig of fresh thyme	sprig of fresh thyme
sprig of fresh parsley	sprig of fresh parsley
1 bay leaf	1 bay leaf
10 black peppercorns	10 black peppercorns

Cover the bones and meat with cold water and bring to the boil. Skim off the froth and scum and cook for 2 hours (pressure cook for 25 minutes). Add the vegetables, washed, trimmed and coarsely chopped and simmer for another 2 hours. Strain, cool and remove the solidified fat.

Court-Bouillon

Used for poaching fish and to make soups and sauces.

Metric/Imperial	American
2 small onions	2 small onions
2 small carrots	2 small carrots
1 bay leaf	1 bay leaf
sprig of fresh tarragon	sprig of fresh tarragon
sprig of fresh parsley	sprig of fresh parsley
6 black peppercorns	6 black peppercorns
juice of ½ lemon	juice of ½ lemon
850 ml/1½ pints water	3¼ cups water

Wash, trim and chop the vegetables. Put all the ingredients in a large pan and bring to the boil. Simmer for 30 minutes. Strain.

Chicken Stock

A pale, golden coloured stock with an excellent flavour ideal for making vegetable soups. It is also the basic stock for all chicken, rabbit and white meat dishes.

Metric/Imperial	American
1 chicken carcase and giblets	1 chicken carcase and giblets
2½ litres/4 pints water	10 cups water
1 onion	1 onion
1 leek	1 leek
1 carrot	1 carrot
sprig of fresh thyme	sprig of fresh thyme
sprig of fresh parsley	sprig of fresh parsley
1 bay leaf	1 bay leaf
10 black peppercorns	10 black peppercorns

Put all the bones and giblets in a large pan. Cover with water, bring to the boil and skim off the froth and scum. Wash and trim the vegetables, leaving their skins intact. Roughly chop and add to the pan. Toss in the herbs and black peppercorns and simmer gently for 2 hours until well reduced. Take off the heat and strain into a bowl, pressing the vegetables to extract all the liquid. When cool, cover and place in a refrigerator. The fat will solidify and can then be easily lifted off with a blunt knife.

SAUCES

Basic White Sauce

Metric/Imperial	American
15 g/½ oz unsalted butter	1½ tbsps sweet butter
15 ml/1 tbsp sunflower oil	1½ tbsps sunflower oil
25 g/1 oz plain flour (wholewheat or un-bleached white)	1½ tbsps all-purpose flour (wholewheat or un-bleached white)
425 ml/15 fl oz milk	1¾ cups milk

Heat the butter and oil together in a saucepan. Stir in the flour and cook for 2-3 minutes. Remove from the heat and gradually add the milk, stirring well after each addition. Return to the heat and bring to the boil, stirring continuously as the sauce thickens.

For everyday dishes and pie fillings I use a wholewheat flour but I prefer to use an unbleached white flour for more elegant dishes whose appearance can be spoilt by the brown bran flecks found in wholewheat flours.

Variations:

Cheese Sauce: add 100 g/4 oz (1 cup) of grated cheese and a pinch of mustard powder and cayenne pepper to the thickened sauce.

Parsley Sauce: before serving stir in 45 ml/3 tbsps fresh parsley.

Devilled Onion Sauce: sauté 2 sliced onions in 15 ml/1 tbsp butter and 30 ml/2 tbsps sunflower oil until soft, being careful not to brown. Follow the basic recipe, i.e. stir in the flour and add the milk as above. Then stir in 5 ml/1 tsp Dijon mustard before serving. A little extra milk may be needed if the sauce becomes too thick.

Bechamel Sauce

Metric/Imperial	*American*
575 ml/1 pint milk	2½ cups milk
2 slices of onion	2 slices of onion
10 black peppercorns	10 black peppercorns
1 bay leaf	1 bay leaf
40 g/1½ oz unsalted butter	3-4 tbsps sweet butter
40 g/1½ oz plain flour (brown or white)	3-4 tbsps all-purpose flour (brown or white)
pinch of grated nutmeg	pinch of grated nutmeg

Put the milk, onion, peppercorns and bay leaf in a pan. Bring to the boil. Remove from the heat and leave to stand for 10-15 minutes. Strain and discard the vegetables and seasonings. Wipe the pan clean and melt the butter over a gentle heat. Stir in the flour and cook for 2-3 minutes. Remove from the heat and gradually add the milk, stirring well after each addition. Return to the heat and bring to the boil, stirring as it begins to thicken. Season with a little nutmeg.

Napolitana Sauce

Metric/Imperial	*American*
30 ml/2 tbsps olive oil	2-3 tbsps olive oil
1 onion, thinly sliced	1 onion, thinly sliced
1 clove garlic, peeled and crushed	1 clove garlic, peeled and crushed
10 ml/1 dessertsp wholewheat flour	1 tbsp wholewheat flour
45 ml/3 tbsps water	3-4 tbsps water
450 g/1 lb ripe tomatoes, chopped	1 lb ripe tomatoes, chopped
1 bay leaf	1 bay leaf
2.5 ml/½ tsp dried oregano	½ tsp dried oregano
2.5 ml/½ tsp dried basil	½ tsp dried basil
freshly ground black pepper	freshly ground black pepper

Heat the olive oil in a saucepan and lightly fry the onion and garlic until soft. Stir in the flour and cook for 2-3 minutes. Add the water, tomatoes, bay leaf, oregano and basil. Season to taste with black pepper. Bring to the boil and simmer gently for 10 minutes. Blend or liquidise until smooth.

Serve with any type of pasta. It is also good with vegetables, rissoles and nut roasts.

Peanut Sauce

Metric/Imperial	American
100 g/4 oz creamed coconut, grated	¼ lb creamed coconut, grated
275 ml/10 fl oz water	1¼ cups water
100 g/4 oz peanuts, ground	1 cup ground peanuts
5 ml/1 tsp turmeric	1 tsp turmeric
5 ml/1 tsp curry powder	1 tsp curry powder
5 ml/1 tsp cayenne pepper	1 tsp cayenne pepper
15-30ml/1-2 tbsps lemon juice	1½-3 tbsps lemon juice

Place the creamed coconut and water in a pan and heat gently until blended. Pour the 'coconut milk' into a liquidiser and add all the remaining ingredients EXCEPT for the lemon juice. Blend until smooth and creamy. Add the lemon juice to taste. Heat through.

Serve hot with vegetables or pasta or cold with a dish of crudités. I also like it hot with a firm, white fish such as monkfish or rock salmon.

Pesto

Metric/Imperial	American
15 ml/1 tbsp fresh basil	1½ tbsps fresh basil
1 clove garlic	1 clove garlic
30 ml/2 tbsps pine kernels	2-3 tbsps pine kernels (pignoli)
5 ml/1 tsp dried basil	1 tsp dried basil
25 g/1 oz Parmesan cheese	1½ tbsps Parmesan cheese
15 ml/1 tbsp olive oil	1½ tbsps olive oil

Chop the fresh basil, garlic and pine kernels. Add the dried basil and pound in a mortar until smooth. Stir in the Parmesan cheese. Gradually add the olive oil, mixing well after each addition until the pesto is the consistency of creamed butter.

Pesto is delicious stirred into piping hot pasta; it is especially good with buckwheat spaghetti. It adds a certain 'je ne sais quoi' to minestrone soup.

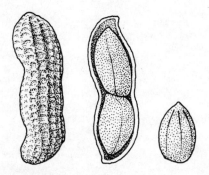

Home-Made Mustard

Metric/Imperial	American
45 ml/3 tbsps mustard powder	3-4 tbsps mustard powder
freshly ground black pepper	freshly ground black pepper
7 ml/1½ tsps white wine vinegar	1½ tsps white wine vinegar
7 ml/1½ tsps groundnut oil	1½ tsps peanut oil

Blend the mustard to a stiff paste with a little water. Add the other ingredients, and mix together thoroughly.

SALAD DRESSINGS

Vinaigrette

Metric/Imperial	American
1 clove garlic, peeled and crushed	1 clove garlic, peeled and crushed
15 ml/1 tbsp white wine vinegar	1½ tbsps white wine vinegar
15 ml/1 tbsp lemon juice	1½ tbsps lemon juice
5 ml/1 tsp Dijon mustard	1 tsp Dijon mustard
75 ml/5 tbsps olive oil	6-7 tbsps olive oil
freshly ground black pepper	freshly ground black pepper

Place the garlic, wine vinegar, lemon juice and mustard in a bowl. Gradually beat in the olive oil until well blended. Season to taste with black pepper.

Walnut and Orange Dressing

Metric/Imperial	American
60 ml/4 tbsps walnut oil	5-6 tbsps walnut oil
30 ml/2 tbsps fresh orange juice	2-3 tbsps fresh orange juice
freshly ground black pepper	freshly ground black pepper

Blend all the ingredients together.

Lemon Dressing

Metric/Imperial
60 ml/4 tbsps groundnut
   oil
30 ml/2 tbsps lemon juice
freshly ground black
   pepper

American
5-6 tbsps peanut oil
2-3 tbsps lemon juice
freshly ground black
   pepper

Blend the oil and lemon juice together and season to taste with black pepper.

Sesame Cream Dressing

Metric/Imperial
30 ml/2 tbsps tahini
30 ml/2 tbsps natural
   yoghurt
1 clove garlic, peeled and
   crushed
15 ml/1 tbsp lemon juice

American
2-3 tbsps tahini
2-3 tbsps unflavored yogurt
1 clove garlic, peeled and
   crushed
1½ tbsps lemon juice

Blend together well.
Delicious with rice salads, and a good dip to serve with crudités.

Minted Yoghurt Dressing

Metric/Imperial
175 ml/6 fl oz natural
   yoghurt
15 ml/1 tbsp lemon juice
1.25 ml/¼ tsp grated
   lemon rind
15 ml/1 tbsp fresh mint,
   chopped

American
¾ cup unflavored yogurt
1½ tbsps lemon juice
¼ tsp grated lemon rind
1½ tbsps fresh mint,
   chopped

Blend together well.

Recipe Index

General Index

Making Your Own Paté

Joyce Van Doorn

Pâté is a savoury mixture of meat, poultry, pulses or fish, sometimes covered with a pastry crust. This book mostly consists of mouth-watering recipes from around the world including dishes not normally described as pâtés in Great Britain such as terrines, mousses, gallantines, rillets, pies and flans.

Author

Joyce van Doorn is a lecturer, writer and broadcaster.

8″ x 8″, 120 pages
Full colour photographic cover
25 line drawings
ISBN 0 907061 01 X   Hardback £5.95
ISBN 0 907061 02 8   Paperback £2.95

Making Your Own Preserves

Jane & Rob Avery

A comprehensive book of over 150 recipes with careful instructions and all the essential background.

Contents

1 Methods, Advantages and Scope
2 General Principles
3 Equipment and Materials
4 Bottling
5 Conserves and Syrups
6 Jams and Jellies
7 Curds, Cheeses and Butters
8 Marmalades, Mincemeats and Crystalized Fruits
9 Pickles and Chutneys
10 Sauces, Vegetable Juices and Vinegars
11 Salting and Drying
12 Meat, Fish and Shellfish

Authors

Rob and Jane Avery are freelance writers specialising in fishing, self-sufficiency and cookery topics.

8″ x 8″, 120 pages
Full colour photographic cover
Numerous line drawings
ISBN 0 907061 17 6   Hardback £6.95
ISBN 0 907061 18 4   Paperback £2.95

The Bread Book

Debbie Boater

A very basic book with fundamental information about the important role that bread plays in our diet and how to make it in its original, nutritious, wholesome form. A wide variety of recipes are included which cover breads, savoury breads, sweet breads, flat breads, pancakes, muffins and pastries.

Author

Debbie Boater is a teacher and founder of the Wholefood School of Nutrition.

8″ x 8″, 96 pages
Full photographic cover
25 line drawings
ISBN 0 904727 95 5   Hardback £5.95
ISBN 0 904727 96 3   Paperback £2.95

Bean Cuisine

Janet Horsley

Bean Cuisine is a comprehensive guide to the cooking of beans and pulses, useful both as a reference book and as a recipe book.

An introductory chapter traces the historic, economic and nutritional aspects of bean cooking, and explains how to use them to make well balanced, nutritious meals. An illustrated A-Z is included to aid recognition, as well as all the information needed to prepare, cook, freeze and sprout the beans.

Author

Janet Horsley is a cookery and nutrition lecturer.

8″ x 8″ 96 pages
Illustrated with line drawings
Full colour photographic cover
ISBN 0 907061 32 X   Hardback £6.95
ISBN 0 907061 33 8   Paperback £2.95

Making Your Own Liqueurs

Joyce van Doorn

With the help of some simple equipment: a set of scales, glassware, a filter and a mixture of herbs, spices, flowers, fruits, sugar and alcohol, you can make your own liqueurs which will be as exotic and tasty as the commercial varieties. Over 200 different recipes are listed ranging from fruits in alcohol, ratafias, herb and flower liqueurs, to bitters and elixirs.

Author

Joyce van Doorn is a lecturer, writer and broadcaster.

8" x 8 ", 120 pages
Full colour photographic cover
65 line drawings
ISBN 0 907061 03 6   Hardback £5.95
ISBN 0 907061 04 4   Paperback £2.95

Tea

Eelco Hesse

Tea drinking originated in China and Japan more than 2000 years ago. This book recounts the fascinating history of tea drinking and the colourful development of the Tea Trade over the centuries.

The author also examines the tools of tea making and how tea is grown and processed throughout the world. There is a section on tea blending and full instructions on making a 'perfect cup of tea'. The appendices contain anecdotes, songs and poetry about tea as well as useful addresses for further information and obtaining supplies.

Author

Eelco Hesse is a well-known authority on tea and the tea trade.

8″ x 8″, 120 pages
Full colour photographic cover
Numerous line drawings and engravings
ISBN 0 907061 05 2   Hardback £6.95
ISBN 0 907061 06 0   Paperback £2.95

Winemaking Month by Month

Brian Leverett

"If you enjoy making wines as well as drinking them you wil find this book both informative and enjoyable. It gives recipes for each month, according to what is in season as well as general guidance on home brewing"
Birmingham Post
"Useful, readable and logically presented."
Do-It-Yourself Magazine

Author

Brian Leverett is a lecturer, journalist and broadcaster.

8″ x 8″, 120 pages
Full colour photographic cover
37 line drawings and tables
ISBN 0 904727 93 9   Hardback £5.95
ISBN 0 904727 94 7   Paperback £2.95

Home Beermaking

Brian Leverett

This book is more than just a collection of recipes with instructions. It explains clearly, with straightforward diagrams, the complex brewing process and how to achieve the best possible results at home, whether from a can or with the traditional ingredients. The unique fault finder chart will help you overcome many of the problems that you may have had with previous attempts at home brewing.

Author

Brian Leverett is a lecturer, journalist and broadcaster.

8″ X 8″, 120 pages
Full colour photographic cover
32 line drawings and tables
ISBN 0 907061 07 9 Hardback £5.95
ISBN 0 907061 08 7 Paperback £2.95